Cambridge Elements

Elements in Rethinking Byzantium
edited by
Leonora Neville
University of Wisconsin-Madison
Darlene Brooks Hedstrom
Brandeis University

SAILING AWAY FROM BYZANTIUM TOWARD EAST ROMAN HISTORY

Leonora Neville
University of Wisconsin-Madison

CAMBRIDGE
UNIVERSITY PRESS

Shaftesbury Road, Cambridge CB2 8EA, United Kingdom

One Liberty Plaza, 20th Floor, New York, NY 10006, USA

477 Williamstown Road, Port Melbourne, VIC 3207, Australia

314–321, 3rd Floor, Plot 3, Splendor Forum, Jasola District Centre,
New Delhi – 110025, India

103 Penang Road, #05–06/07, Visioncrest Commercial, Singapore 238467

Cambridge University Press is part of Cambridge University Press & Assessment,
a department of the University of Cambridge.

We share the University's mission to contribute to society through the pursuit of
education, learning and research at the highest international levels of excellence.

www.cambridge.org
Information on this title: www.cambridge.org/9781009595551

DOI: 10.1017/9781009595582

© Leonora Neville 2025

This publication is in copyright. Subject to statutory exception and to the provisions
of relevant collective licensing agreements, no reproduction of any part may take
place without the written permission of Cambridge University Press & Assessment.

When citing this work, please include a reference to the DOI 10.1017/9781009595582

First published 2025

A catalogue record for this publication is available from the British Library

ISBN 978-1-009-59555-1 Hardback
ISBN 978-1-009-59554-4 Paperback
ISSN 3033-4292 (online)
ISSN 3033-4284 (print)

Cambridge University Press & Assessment has no responsibility for the persistence
or accuracy of URLs for external or third-party internet websites referred to in this
publication and does not guarantee that any content on such websites is, or will remain,
accurate or appropriate.

For EU product safety concerns, contact us at Calle de José Abascal, 56, 1°, 28003
Madrid, Spain, or email eugpsr@cambridge.org

Sailing Away from Byzantium toward East Roman History

Elements in Rethinking Byzantium

DOI: 10.1017/9781009595582
First published online: June 2025

Leonora Neville
University of Wisconsin-Madison
Author for correspondence: Leonora Neville, Leonora.neville@wisc.edu

Abstract: Although the first thing one learns about the "Byzantine Empire" is that it was really the eastern Roman Empire, scholars have preferred to call it "Byzantine" in a repudiation of the self-conception and emic vocabulary of the inhabitants of that polity. The terminology of "Byzantium" artificially severs the "medieval" eastern Roman Empire from its "classical" roots allowing for the fundamentally Eurocentric schematization of history into "ancient," "medieval," and "Renaissance" periods. "Byzantine" is not a benign term of art but has served a variety of political and historiographical agendas, including maintaining nationalist visions of ethnic continuity, creating precedents for communism, enabling politics of nostalgia for Orthodox dominion, and constructing visions of western European superiority and masculinity that justify colonialism. By exploring these intellectual legacies of "Byzantium," and the benefits of conceptualizing Roman history as an unsevered whole, this Element exhorts scholars to let go of the "Byzantine" misnomer.

Keywords: Byzantine, Byzantium, east Roman, later Roman, medieval Roman

© Leonora Neville 2025

ISBNs: 9781009595551 (HB), 9781009595544 (PB), 9781009595582 (OC)
ISSNs: 3033-4292 (online), 3033-4284 (print)

Contents

1 Introduction: Names Matter   1

2 Work Done by "Byzantium"   5

3 Reasons for Change   40

   Conclusions   54

   Bibliography   57

1 Introduction: Names Matter

The history and culture of the later Roman Empire is surprising, thought-provoking, and disruptive. It is rich and rewarding on its own, and marvelously instructive for those facing the many global political and cultural challenges of the twenty-first century. Eastern Roman cultural products, full of wit, literary playfulness, stunning expressiveness, and beauty, provide aesthetic delights and moving reminders of the myriad manifestations of human creativity.

Given all this richness and utility in the subject matter, why is it that later eastern Roman culture is so rarely studied? One obvious answer is that it is called "Byzantine," a term that commonly means obscure, convoluted, malicious, and devious. This derogatory discourse is not grounded in historical reality but serves to silence and occlude a culture that disrupts paradigms of Western supremacy. The disparaging meaning of the word "byzantine" developed in tandem with the negative evaluation of the society so named.

This Element contends that "Byzantium" is not a harmless technical term but an ongoing way to nullify the radical disruptiveness of later Rome. The academic discipline of "Byzantine Studies" addresses a culture and society so disturbing to western European self-conception that its identity and existence needed to be erased. The term "Byzantine Empire" is deployed as a way of denying that the Roman Empire of the Middle Ages was *really* the Roman Empire, hence clearing the way for standard narratives of Western Civilization.

As names, "Byzantium" and "Byzantine" are both inaccurate and insulting. It is inaccurate in that there never was a Byzantine Empire and only a scattering of people ever answered to that name. Byzantium was the name of the ancient city that Constantine refounded in 330 as New Rome, and commonly called Constantinople. Citizens of this town were known in antiquity as Byzantines and that term was occasionally used for people who lived in Constantinople from the fourth century on. It could distinguish citizens of Constantinople from the other Romans. A seventh-century attestation of the term indicates that in some contexts it could also be used to describe eastern Romans as opposed to western Romans.[1] After the Ottoman conquest in 1453, exiles in the West sometimes called themselves "Byzantines," meaning that they were from Constantinople. These occasional premodern usages of "Byzantine" refer to people who in other contexts would be called Romans; it was a rare affectation rather than a common name.[2] The city Constantine founded was the new capital of the Roman state.

---

[1] Theodoropoulos, "Did the Byzantines Call Themselves Byzantines? Elements of Eastern Roman Identity in the Imperial Discourse of the Seventh Century."

[2] The textual evidence from this culture is unanimous and unambiguous in naming its political identity as Roman. Objections to using this culture's own vocabulary for themselves, which will be discussed in Section 3, provoked a full illustration of this basic point in Kaldellis, *Romanland:*

That "Byzantium" was really the continuation of the Roman Empire has never been in dispute. It is usually the first thing one learns about "Byzantium." Similarly, "Byzantine" is nearly always glossed, in introductory uses, with the explanation that the "Byzantines" *thought* they were Roman or *called themselves* Roman, with the strong implication that their belief was mistaken. The choice to use "Byzantine" and "Byzantium" is a rejection of the emic terminology of the society and people being named. It is a fundamental inaccuracy equivalent to calling Louis XIV a Lutetian who thought he was French.[3]

That "Byzantine" is inaccurate terminology is not a new revelation. One of the leading researchers in later Roman history, John Bagnell Bury, called for the term "Byzantine" to be dropped from academic discourse in the late nineteenth century, declaring: "No 'Byzantine Empire' ever began to exist; the Roman Empire did not come to an end until 1453."[4] As he explained:

> Every century of the Roman Empire differed from the preceding and from the succeeding, but the development was continuous; the Empire was still the Roman Empire, and I am not aware that it is usual to give a man a new name when he enters upon a new decade of life. We designate a man as young and old; and so we may speak of the earlier and later ages of a kingdom or an empire. But *Byzantine* is a proper adjective and is too apparently precise not to be misleading.[5]

It is not the case, therefore, that scholars since the turn of the millennium have discovered suddenly that "Byzantine" is an inaccurate term. We have known this all along, but we have chosen to use it anyway.

Calling people by the name that they want to use for themselves is a fundamental aspect of respect. If I tell you my name is Leonora, and you insist on calling me Lorraine, it indicates a lack of respect for me as a person and

---

Ethnicity and Empire in Byzantium. On the role of cultural memory in maintaining Roman identity, see Neville, *Heroes and Romans in Twelfth-Century Byzantium*, 1–7, 195–206. On the construction of east Roman loyalty, see Ando, *Imperial Ideology and Provincial Loyalty in the Roman Empire*. On shifting conceptions of Hellenism, see Kaldellis, *Hellenism in Byzantium*. While Kaldellis has been the field's most vocal defender of our subject's Roman identity, he has not been alone. See, for example, Whalin, *Roman Identity from the Arab Conquests to the Triumph of Orthodoxy*; Aschenbrenner and Ransohoff, eds., *The Invention of Byzantium in Early Modern Europe*; Stewart, Parnell, and Whately, eds., *The Routledge Handbook on Identity in Byzantium*. I have urged my colleagues to take the logical step of abandoning the terminology of "Byzantium": *Is it Time to De-Colonize the Terms Byzantine & Byzantium*, video discussion, Fordham University, October 4, 2021, www.medievalists.net/2021/10/decolonize-terms-byzantine-byzantium/; *Byzantium and Friends*, Anthony Kaldellis, host, "Is it time to abandon the rubric 'Byzantium'? with Leonora Neville," episode 43, February 11, 2021, www.medievalists.net/2021/02/abandon-rubric-byzantium-leonora-neville/; Kaldellis, *The Case for East Roman Studies*, 8.

[3] Paris was once Lutetia Parisiorum. [4] Bury, *A History of the Later Roman Empire*, v.
[5] Bury, *A History of the Later Roman Empire*, vi.

negates a part of my self-determination.[6] Likewise, if someone tells you she is a Ho-Chunk Indian, insisting that she is really a Winnebago Native American is condescending and insulting.

Beyond the lack of civility in rejecting a society's own naming practices, the term "Byzantine" is pejorative because that word has negative meanings deriving from prejudicial and derogatory interpretations of later Roman society. In English, "byzantine" is an adjective used to describe convoluted, impenetrable impediments to progress and action. The *Oxford English Dictionary* explains explicitly that the negative meaning of the word arises out of perceptions of eastern Rome: "Byzantine: Reminiscent of the manner, style, or spirit of Byzantine politics; intricate, complicated; inflexible, rigid, unyielding."[7] "Byzantine" is used to describe things that thwart progress and dreams. Newspaper headlines proclaim: "Byzantine water laws will leave Californians high and dry"[8] or "Byzantine Boston makes it next to impossible to open a restaurant."[9] Lapses in appropriate medical care are attributed to California's "byzantine system for allocating care."[10] The president of the American Medical Association criticized health insurance plans' "byzantine system of authorization controls."[11] People are frustrated by "byzantine and elaborate regulations."[12]

As well as causing headaches, "byzantine" systems prevent the fair exercise of justice. An inmate abused in a prison was thwarted by "restrictive grievance procedures" that "created these Byzantine administrative processes that are just designed to eventually make a prisoner fail to take one of the steps so they give up and can't bring a lawsuit."[13] The story of a family forced to great misfortune by Medicaid rules shows "just how Byzantine this system is for people and how draining it could be both emotionally and financially." A commentator on this

---

[6] Saying that Lorraine thinks she's Leonora doesn't make it better.
[7] *Oxford English Dictionary*, s.v. "Byzantine (*adj.*), sense 2," September 2023, https://doi.org/10.1093/OED/1060543963.
[8] Frank and Domus, "Byzantine Water Laws Will Leave Californians High and Dry."
[9] "Byzantine Boston Makes It Next to Impossible to Open a Restaurant," *Boston Globe*.
[10] Sharp, "Gaps in Care for Eating Disorders; Cases Have Surged, but Long Waits and Byzantine Medi-Cal Rules Stymie the State's Poorest Patients."
[11] Solomon, "Prior Authorization Increases Use of Health Care Resources, Physicians Say."
[12] "One Part of British Culture That Didn't Cross the Ocean to America; I'm Amazed How Compliant the Brits Are with Byzantine Regulations Imposed by Their Leaders," *Wall Street Journal (Online)*. Mellow, "Disaster Insurance Gets Lift in Emerging Markets." Quite apart from the historical issue at hand, the derogatory "byzantine" discourse denigrates the work of government itself. Like a slowly dripping acid, the laments over the "byzantine" evils of government administration erode trust in the public institutions that ameliorate the viciousness of raw capitalism and discourage support for large-scale collective infrastructures that work toward a more humane society.
[13] Mealins, "Lawsuit Claims Correctional Officers Stabbed, Beat Inmate: TDOC: Wounds Were Self-Inflicted, Accidental."

story concurred: "Byzantine is such a good word for it."[14] Brittney Griner survived the "byzantine Russian legal system."[15] NCAA student athletes are unable to receive compensation because the NCAA has "a byzantine set of rules."[16] Special education students fight "a byzantine puzzle of laws."[17] "Byzantine" is also used of dangerous, clandestine, unclear situations. Yevgeny Prigozhin's abortive coup attempt against Valdimir Putin was described by the journalist Christiane Amanpour as "very byzantine. These are two ... essential gangsters fighting for supremacy and money and power."[18] A national security analyst said of trying to understand contemporary Russian politics: "You know, it's a very byzantine situation whenever you're trying to figure out what's going on ... inside the Kremlin."[19]

While this Element focuses on the English language traditions, other European languages also use "byzantine" as a derogatory term, albeit with different implications. As Przemysław Marciniak explains: "The definitions in other languages are similar, describing Byzantinism as a tendency for hair-splitting (Dutch), excessively ceremonial and slavish behaviour (German), for endless and purposeless debates (French, Italian) and even for hypocrisy and the presentation of the bad as good (Polish), therefore mostly focusing on the Byzantine (mis-)behaviour."[20] While traditions differ on what precisely is wrong with "byzantine," there is a remarkable international consensus that it is deplorable.

Like the inaccuracy of the term, the derogatory meaning of "byzantine" has been known and acknowledged by scholars for well over a century. Bury argued that discarding the term Byzantine is advantageous because "[s]o many prejudicial associations have grown up round this inauspicious word that it almost involves a *petitio principii,* like the phrase *Bas-Empire* in French."[21] Bury's case against "Byzantine" was not so much refuted as ignored. His history was widely cited as authoritative for decades after its publication, so this is not a case of a brilliant but obscure outlier who never found widespread recognition. Rather he was among the most prominent scholarly voices in an international field.

---

[14] Brown et al., "PBS NewsHour for December 26, 2023."
[15] Field Level Media, "Brittney Griner Plans 'intimate, Moving' Memoir on Imprisonment in Russia."
[16] Berkowitz, "NCAA Facing New 'pay-for-Play' Challenges in Lawsuit."
[17] Fritze, "Special Ed Student Can Sue School: Supreme Court Ruling Could Empower Parents."
[18] Amanpour and Isaacson, "Interview with Former U.S. Ambassador to NATO and Former U.S. Special Representative for Ukraine Negotiations Kurt Volker. Aired 1-2p ET."
[19] After explaining that the question posed could not be answered, the interviewer summarized: "Yes. Byzantine, as you said." Steve Hall, interviewed by Michael Holmes: Holmes et al., "Pro-War Russian Blogger Killed in Explosion."
[20] Marciniak, "Oriental Like Byzantium", 48.
[21] Bury, *A History of the Later Roman Empire*, viii.

The communities of scholars who were becoming known as "Byzantinists" chose to ignore Bury's case and persisted in using the term "Byzantine" while knowing that it was inaccurate and derogatory. In 1900, Fredrick Harrison acknowledged both the mistakenness and pejorative nature of "byzantine," saying: "the only accurate name for this [state] is the 'Empire of New Rome,'" and "prejudice remains so strong it may be as well to avoid the term 'Byzantine Empire.'"[22] Yet rather than follow through with his own suggestion to drop the term, he pivots without explanation to say "it is inevitable to speak of Byzantine history, or art, or civilization, when we refer to that which had its seat on the Bosporus."[23] What is the source of this inevitability? What prompted Harrison, and subsequent generations of scholars, to continue using a terminology that they knew was false and insulting? The following section attempts to provide some answers to this question.

2 Work Done by "Byzantium"

Nearly all scholars would agree that they share a fundamental obligation to be as truthful, accurate, and fair-minded as possible. Methodologies for achieving these goals can vary widely in different eras and fields, but it's fair to say that people who dedicate their lives to learning are motivated to clarify rather than obfuscate their subjects of study. Using the inaccurate and derogatory term "Byzantine," therefore, must have provided some benefits or advantages to scholars that outweighed its problems. To understand what motivated scholars to use it, we need to examine the various kinds of work the term has done, and in some cases, continues to do.

The interests and agendas discussed in the following pages had varying levels of value and significance for scholars working in different eras and cultures. A good many scholars cared not at all for some of these projects, and a great deal about others. Many now think of these agendas as things of the past that no longer impact our scholarship. Yet, before we can debate the degree of our independence from the histories of our field, we need to confront and reflect on those histories.

There is considerable variety in the major functions that have made the "Byzantine" usage appealing. A commonality is a preference to see the history of the distant past as having "Byzantines" in it rather than Romans. Scholars over the centuries were variously engaged in the process of creating a usable past that would inform their present society and culture with the proper lessons of history. The history that was desired for these projects contained a "Byzantine" Empire,

---

[22] Harrison, *Byzantine History*, 47.   [23] Harrison, *Byzantine History*, 47.

implying that something about a history with a longer Roman Empire was undesirable.

I see the work done by "Byzantine" as falling into three broad categories, each with a number of different subsets. One category has to do with making later Roman history fit within a broad theory of human difference based in race and blood-borne nationality. The idea that Greek people could have descendants who were Romans is difficult to accommodate within a racial understanding of humanity, which motivates denial of Roman identity. Within this category, "Byzantine" functions largely as something to call these people other than "Roman." Another category is the use of "Byzantine" as precedents for communism and Orthodox Imperialism. The final category comprises ways that "Byzantium" helped support ideas of western European superiority. "Byzantium" is essential for getting eastern Roman history out of the way and allowing traditional narratives of the rise of the "West" to be plausible. Here "Byzantium" is a denial of Roman institutional and cultural continuity that separates West from the East and gives primacy to the turning points of Western progress. "Byzantium" has also served as a foil for the construction and teaching of a dominating, active, and western masculinity that helped make western domination of the world seem natural.

Myths of Racial Continuity

Abundant evidence shows, beyond any reasonable doubt, that the vast majority of people living in the territory of the Roman Empire in the Middle Ages were, in their own self-conception, Romans. This means that somehow over fifteen centuries the people who had identified as Hellenes, Phrygians, Macedonians, among others, had descendants who were Romans. If one holds that communities are constituted by shared ideas about who they are, this was more than enough time for a group identity to shift. It is interesting, but hardly impossible, that after multiple generations, the lineal descendants of Greeks could be Romans. After all, the United States is full of people who are Americans whose ancestors were not. Within only a few generations many people move from being foreign immigrants to hyphenated Polish-Americans, for example, to people with only vague familial memories of other past identities. In this process, the self-definition of individuals and communities makes those identities true and accurate descriptions of who they are. While commonplace now, this understanding of the constitutive power of community self-conception marks a significant departure from theories of human difference that were prevalent in the nineteenth and much of the twentieth centuries.

The idea that all humans were members of different races, or a mixture of races, took hold in the late eighteenth century and became increasingly entrenched in politics, culture, and society. Proven definitively false through the study of the human genome in the twenty-first century, and morally repugnant earlier through the racially motivated genocides of the twentieth century, the conceptualization of humans as belonging to different races has been one of the most destructive of humanity's bad ideas.[24] Yet this was the most prevalent and influential way of thinking about human difference for nearly two centuries.

Within a nineteenth-century racially based understanding of humanity, the proposition that the Greek speaking denizens of the eastern Roman Empire turned into Romans is simply nonsensical. In this theory, a Greek was a Greek because he was biologically a Greek. If various accidents of culture led this Greek to believe that he was a Roman, he was simply wrong. This belief in the essential variances of different peoples based on their biology certainly contributed to the refusal to call medieval Romans, Romans. Within this system, culture, beliefs, social relationships, and actions are not enough to change people from Greeks into Romans, and then from Romans back into Greeks: Whatever the later Romans thought they were, they must have been wrong, because they used to be Greeks.

The struggle of nationalist Greeks against the Ottoman Empire was one of the great test cases both of national ideology and racial theory in the nineteenth century. Idealistic western Europeans, believing that nations rightly should have freedom of self-government, fought alongside Greek nationalists trying to gain independence from the Ottomans. This movement was fired, in part, by the desire to rescue the descendants of the glorious ancient Greeks from modern subjugation. It was taken as obvious that these Greeks of the 1820s were the same "people" as the Greeks who produced Homer and Demosthenes, and this continuity mattered a great deal to those fighting for Greek freedom.

Racial theory was never merely a way of describing human difference but was constantly engaged in comparative evaluations of the variously imagined benefits and defects of different races. Some races were considered better than others. Assigning a group to a racial category imputed to all members of that group certain mental, physical, and moral qualities. Prejudicial thinking became realism. The philhellenes of the 1820s believed they fought to save a great and noble people from the Ottomans.

This vision of Greek continuity was contested by Jacob Fallmerayer, who in 1830 published a history of Morea, in which he argued that the original Greek inhabitants had been replaced by Slav, Albanian, and Turkish peoples in the so-called age of migrations of the early Middle Ages. His negative judgment is abundantly clear in the opening sentence of his preface:

---

[24] Appiah, *The Lies That Bind*.

> The race of the Hellenes has been wiped out in Europe. Physical beauty, intellectual brilliance, innate harmony and simplicity, art, competition, city, village, the splendour of column and temple – indeed, even the name has disappeared from the surface of the Greek continent . . . . Not the slightest drop of undiluted Hellenic blood flows in the veins of the Christian population of present-day Greece.[25]

In his conception, the glories of ancient Greece were due to the racial characteristics of the ancient Greeks. Classical Greece had been splendid because the ancient Greeks were a good race, but nineteenth-century Morea, he asserted, did not have splendor because the current inhabitants were from different, far inferior, races.

The association of the ancient Greeks with a good race, or a particularly good subspecies within the Caucasian race, lay behind the great offense taken by Greek nationalists and European philhellenes at the suggestion that the modern Greeks were actually Slavs and Albanians. The tremendous furor provoked by Fallmerayer's theory makes sense only in the context of widespread acceptance of racial theories of history. Within this system, it was plausible that one racial group could replace another. If Fallmerayer were right, the people living in nineteenth-century Greek-speaking territories of the Ottoman Empire might not really be Greeks after all.

The philhellene refutation of Fallmerayer disputed the facts on the ground rather than the underlying theory. George Finlay, one of the Englishmen who joined the fight for Greek independence, produced a comprehensive *History of Greece (From Its Conquest by the Romans to the Present Time, B.C. 146 to A.D. 1864)*, which sought to demonstrate the continuous history of the Greek people from antiquity to modern times. He believed that racial change took place and indeed was one of the most important aspects of history, arguing that "no subject connected with the decline and fall of the Roman empire, both in the East and West, [is] of greater importance for tracing accurately the political and social progress of the inhabitants of Europe, than the history of the diminution, extinction, and modification of the population in the various nations subjected to the Roman domination."[26] He differed from Fallmerayer, however, in holding that the Greek population was still present. He dealt with the arguments for change brought forth by Fallmerayer by accepting that the *Thracians* had been replaced by Slavs, while insisting on the continuity of the Greek people:

---

[25] Fallmerayer, *Geschichte der Halbinsel Morea während des Mittelalters: ein historischer Versuch*, iii.
[26] Finlay, *History*, 3: 224.

> No historical facts seem more evident than these two, that the Thracian race – which during the first century of the Christian era formed the most numerous ethnological division of the inhabitants of the eastern part of the Roman empire – has long ceased to exist; and, on the other hand, that the modern Greeks are a modification of the ancient Achaian, Dorian, Ionian, Aeolian, and Hellenic population.[27]

He acknowledged that movements of peoples had led to the extinction of certain human groups, just not that of the ancient Greeks. Finlay stressed the continuity in both Greek genetics and political spirit that persisted through centuries of historical change.

While Fallmerayer took it as a tragedy of history that the true Greeks had been replaced by Slavs and Albanians, considerable numbers of people who identified with those latter categories thought the expansion of their people was a good thing. While rejecting his extremely prejudicial denigration of Slavic people, they accepted the historical argument that much of the European provinces of the Ottoman Empire had been thoroughly settled by their ancestors. In the context of the decline of the Ottoman Empire and the Balkan wars of the late- and early twentieth centuries, this was an obviously political fight over whether the Greeks, Bulgarians, or Albanians had a natural right to self-governance of Ottoman territory. Studies of archaeology and linguistics that attempted to trace the movements of people in the "age of migrations" became highly contested with scholars aligning with different nationalist camps making claims for the absence or presence of Slavs and Greeks. Nineteenth-century Russian intellectuals posited that not only Thrace and Hellas had been settled by Slavs, but also most of Anatolia. They credited this Slavic migration with saving the eastern Roman Empire, a theory which paved the way for the utopian visions of natural Slavic communism to be discussed in the following section.

All the intellectual combatants in this fight stood on the same epistemological foundation that human races were different. Greeks and Slavs, for them, were not identities born of common language, culture, and religion, but different kinds of human. For Greek nationalists and philhellenes of the nineteenth century, the Greeks had always been Greeks. They could readily admit that the "Byzantines" *thought* they were Romans, but because that view could not be squared with their scientific theories, the medieval people who thought they were Romans were dismissed as wrong. Politically, they needed the Romans to be Greeks, and intellectually, they did not believe that the Roman identity was anything other than false consciousness or mistaken belief.

---

[27] Finlay, *History*, 3:225.

If you want Greeks now to be the same people as the Greeks of classical Athens, it is very inconvenient if they were Romans for fifteen centuries. The project of Greek nationalism is aided by the vagueness of the "Byzantine" terminology, which allows the "Byzantines" to remain simply Greeks who believed, mistakenly, that they were Romans. Given that the emic vocabulary of "Roman" could not be accepted as valid within this worldview, there was no disadvantage of inaccuracy in using "Byzantine." Since those people didn't know who they were anyway, their self-describing terminology was not accurate, and so could be dismissed. Scholars could believe that the people who called themselves Romans were actually Greeks, or Slavs, or Albanians, as they saw fit. The term "Byzantine" usefully swept the medieval Greeks' embarrassing mistake under the rug by allowing scholars and their audiences to more easily ignore that these people had mistakenly thought they were Roman.

Furthermore, the lasting vagueness as to what particular ethnic and racial groups it referred to made "Byzantine" particularly useful in glossing over scholarly disagreements about the ethnic history of the Middle Ages. As a substitute for the emic vocabulary of "Roman," "Byzantine" gave free rein to various visions of ethnic continuity. Historians could get on with doing the history of the "Byzantines" without waiting for the results of the throwdown fights about whether they were Slavs or Greeks. Colleagues invested in those fights could study the history of the Slavs, Greeks, Armenians, Syrians, Egyptians, and so on under the rubric of "Byzantine" history. "Byzantine," as an artificial technical name with no historical referent, was a perfect umbrella term for the various ethnic and racial groups that were thought to have coexisted and contended in the Roman east. If an ethnic identity could be imputed to an historical individual, they could be, for example, an Armenian in the Byzantine Empire or a "Byzantine Armenian." If ethnicity was unknown, they could be referred to simply as a "Byzantine."

Finlay articulated clearly this conception of "Byzantium" as a group of distinct nations held together by an overpowering government. He described the "Byzantine" Empire as a political entity containing different, distinct nationalities, rather like the Austro-Hungarian Empire. He listed "Romans, Greeks, Armenians, Isaurians, Lycaonians, Phrygians, Syrians, and Gallo-Grecians" as the races within the empire in the seventh century,[28] and he chided both modern *and medieval* historians for being duped into thinking there was a "Byzantine" nation:

> We perceive that there was no real unity among the people, and yet the unity created by the government was so imposing, that both contemporary and

---

[28] Finlay, *History*, 2:11.

modern historians have treated the history of the Byzantine empire as if it represented the feelings and interests of a Byzantine nation, and almost overlooked the indelible distinctions of the Greek, Armenian, and Sclavonian races, which, while forced into simultaneous action by the great administrative power that ruled them, constantly retained their own, national peculiarities.[29]

In thinking that historians of medieval times were just as guilty as the modern ones of overlooking racial differences, Finlay valued his certain knowledge of racial continuity over the statements of medieval witnesses. This vision of a polity comprised of many different ethnicities allowed for modern nationalist groups to trace the history of their people within the "Byzantine" Empire as separate groups. Finlay could insist both that the "Byzantine" emperors did not alter the Greeks and that "Byzantine" history was part of Greek history precisely because of the semantic malleability of "Byzantine."[30]

Back when the racial theory of human difference was commonly believed to be scientifically true, and hence morally neutral, scholars had no obligation to adopt the nomenclature used by the Romans of the eastern Mediterranean because those names, they believed, were used in error. On the contrary, since the people who thought they were Romans simply were not, then calling them Romans would have been inaccurate. Within a racially inflected epistemology, calling them Romans merely perpetuated their own mistaken beliefs about themselves. Since this group of people did not accurately know who they were, the scholars with this worldview could regard "Byzantine" as an unproblematic, and indeed technically precise, label.

While such racial theories no longer hold a respectable place in the academy, it would be utterly naïve to think that our world has completely transcended race-based ideas of difference. People continue to define themselves with reference to who they think their ancestors were, in ways that can lead to a desire for long-term ethnic continuity. In 1995, when I was studying in Thessaloniki, two students – one Slovenian and one Greek – got into a heated debate over whether Saint Cyril had been a Slav or a Greek. Knowing that I was a presumably neutral American studying "Byzantine history," they appealed to me to settle the matter. My answer, that Cyril was a Roman, was rejected out of hand. They both agreed that "of course he *thought* he was a Roman," but they

---

[29] Finlay, *History of the Byzantine and Greek Empires, from DCCXVI to MCCCCLIII*, 538.
[30] "Still, neither the Roman Caesars, nor the Byzantine emperors, any more than the Frank princes and Turkish sultans, were able to interrupt the continual transmission of a political inheritance by each generation of the Greek race to its successors." Finlay, *History*, 1:xxii. "During this period, the history of the Greeks is closely interwoven with the annals of the Imperial government, so that the history of the Byzantine Empire forms a portion of the history of the Greek nation." Finlay, *History*, 1:viii.

wanted to know what he "really was" and pressed me not to demure from rendering judgment to avoid giving offense. It took quite a while to get them to understand that indeed I truly believed that Cyril was *really* a Roman. They then decided that I was a postmodernist who didn't believe in truth and dismissed everything I said thereafter. While neither of these young scholars held classically racist views, the background radiation of racial theories of humanity remained so strongly embedded that they both knew that the man must have belonged, biologically speaking, to a particular kind of human category, either Greek or Slav. As generations change, this thinking is fading and becoming far less common, but it remains a matter of recent memory and certainly has contemporary adherents.

Precedents for Communism and Orthodox Autocracy

"Byzantine" history has also functioned as an historical precedent for communism. Since the fall of the Soviet Union, this use has declined precipitously, but it was extremely common among some communities for much of the twentieth century. The seeds of this theory were sown in the late nineteenth century among Russian intellectuals who seized upon the idea that the eastern Roman Empire was thoroughly settled with Slavs in the "age of migrations." Vasilij Vasil'evskij (1838–99) took Fallmerayer's thesis in a positive direction, arguing that the large-scale migration of Slavic peoples in the seventh and eighth centuries transformed society by practicing collective ownership of land.[31] The naturally communistic tendencies of the Slavic peasants, he argued, were manifested in the free village communes of the middle "Byzantine" Empire. These free communes of Slavic peasants were protected by the strong hand of the emperor, who suppressed the predations of the aristocracy from the seventh through tenth centuries. During the eleventh century, a new "feudal" aristocracy arose, under German influence, which destroyed the vitality of the Byzantine economy by buying up the village communes and forcing the peasants into a status of servile renters, or *paroikoi*.[32] Within this narrative, the migration of Slavs into the territory of the sixth-century empire saved the Roman state; the alliance of naturally communistic peasants with strong imperial authority led to prosperity for all. From the standpoint of Marxist theory, this represented a Slavic exceptionalism that broke with the progression from slavery to feudalism to capitalism. The theory may also have been appealing in blaming the rise of serfdom in Russia on the Germans.

---

[31] Kazhdan, "Russian Pre-Revolutionary Studies on Eleventh-Century Byzantium," 112.
[32] Kazhdan, "Russian Pre-Revolutionary Studies on Eleventh-Century Byzantium."

In this story, the "Byzantine" state was important as a Slavic state, and hence there was little interest in seeing continuities with earlier phases of Roman history. "Byzantine" history was Slavic, Orthodox, medieval history, functionally disconnected from pre-Slavic and pre-Christian history.

It is easy to see the appeal of this theory, and how it could have been modified and redeployed continuously throughout the era of the Soviet Union. Demonstrating that communism had flourished in the past, and had arisen naturally, provided powerful assurance that communism could work now and in the future. The greatness of the free Slavic peasant communes provided one of the few positive narratives about "Byzantium" in the twentieth century. Not surprisingly, "Byzantine" history was popular and relatively well-funded in the Soviet Union. The history of the autocratic Orthodox, Slavic state, in which peasants flourished, provided an appealing imagined past for Eastern Bloc countries. That the era of peasant prosperity was brought to an end by the creeping influence of the West made it even better. "Byzantine" history was a common topic in secondary school curricula in the twentieth century in the Eastern Bloc. Through the 1990s, I could count on most eastern Europeans to have the free Slavic peasant communes in mind when I mentioned "Byzantine" history.

While far more positive, this narrative shares a high degree of fictionality with the more derogatory theories about "Byzantium." There are a few indications that villages had shared responsibility for paying taxes, but none verify that their land was owned or worked in common. While the imperial government faced a monetary and fiscal crisis in the eleventh century, the great economic collapse that was thought to have been wrought by the destruction of the free village communes did not happen.[33]

"Byzantium" nevertheless remains far more prevalent as a topic of study in Eastern Europe, and especially Russia, than it is in Western Europe and the United States. The old social history of free peasants, however, is no longer a subject of fascination. My dissertation research led to a book on provincial society that is strikingly at odds with the traditional Soviet interpretation, but by the time it was published in 2004, no one was particularly interested in standing up for the old model, and the paradigm shifted without a fight.[34] The Russians of my generation and older whom I meet are not surprised to hear that the Byzantine history of their grade school textbooks was largely a Soviet fantasy.

---

[33] Hendy, "The Economy: A Brief Survey," 141–52; Hendy, *Studies in the Byzantine Monetary Economy, c. 300–1450*; Laiou, *The Economic History of Byzantium from the Seventh through the Fifteenth Century.*

[34] Neville, *Authority in Byzantine Provincial Society, 950–1100.*

In post-Soviet Russia, interest in "Byzantium" functions as a model and precedent, not of natural communism but of an Orthodox, autocratic empire aligned against the West. In this usage, Russia continues the heritage of the great empire that defended Orthodoxy. Vladimir Putin has promoted this vision of Russia as the Third Rome and with it a politics of expansionist Orthodox dominion.[35] This tradition picks up the thread of nineteenth-century Russian imperialism, which also saw Moscow as inheriting the mantle of Constantinople as the defender of Orthodoxy. Because of the reach and impact of Russian state propaganda, this vision of "Byzantium" as a bastion of autocratic Orthodoxy is among the most commonly held contemporary images of "Byzantine" history. This school of thought prefers a history that has "Byzantium" instead of later "Rome" because this distinction creates a politically potent anti-Western past. In the following section, we will discuss in detail how "Byzantium" helps uphold the category of the West. For those who wish to see the world as dominated by an ongoing conflict between West and East, "Byzantium" is a preferred classification.

Beyond its use in contemporary politics, this vision of "Byzantium" as a robustly Orthodox, autocratic, anti-Western society distorts the study of later Roman history by presuming the answers to major social and political questions. For scholars working within this discourse, all aspects of religion that look like modern Orthodoxy are upheld as normative, and all those that do not are ignored. Yet any vision of a fully formed Orthodox theology and religious practice inaugurated by Constantine and existing unchanged through the centuries is a distortion. The plurality, diversity, and change within later Roman religious beliefs, experiences, and practices is muted when these topics are approached with the assumption that they conform to modern Orthodoxy.[36] Furthermore, insofar as it is used to support autocracy and antidemocratic political movements, this discourse of Orthodox empire is problematic for individuals who prize self-determination and open societies.

"Byzantium" and a Worldview of Western Supremacy

A less immediately obvious but nonetheless profound work of "Byzantium" is to get eastern Roman history out of the way of "Western Civilization." As western European scholars developed the dominant (still commonly taught) narrative of Western Civilization, the existence of the medieval Roman Empire

---

[35] Putin, "On the Historical Unity of Russians and Ukrainians"; Dickinson, "Putin's New Ukraine Essay Reveals Imperial Ambitions," www.atlanticcouncil.org/blogs/ukrainealert/putins-new-ukraine-essay-reflects-imperial-ambitions/; Drost and de Graaf, "Putin and the Third Rome," 28–45.

[36] On this see Cameron, *Byzantine Matters*.

needed to be denied. The novel category of "Byzantine" helped to safely erase the reality of the polity's continuity across the notional divides that defined the West. This complex use of "Byzantium" as an aid in constructing valorized narratives of the West contributes to a worldview of Western superiority. It does not call directly for the conquest and colonization of the East – this construction of "Byzantine" history is not a *cause* of colonialism – but it helps create a way of seeing the world in which European domination of the globe seems natural.

As taught in North American high schools and colleges, the story of Western Civilization begins in Greece and ends in Philadelphia. The thread of this narrative starts in classical Athens with Plato, Aristotle, and Pericles. It then winds to Rome, focusing on Italy for several centuries, before moving north with Clovis and Charlemagne and centering firmly over France for most of the Middle Ages, widening to include Germany and Italy in the Renaissance, with coverage expanding to England, Portugal, and the Netherlands with the development of global seafaring empires. The establishment of English colonies in North America allowed for the transference of Western Civilization across the Atlantic and its crowning achievements in the US Constitution. Thence Western Civilization expanded across the entire North American continent and, through various European empires, across the globe. There is no place for eastern Roman history and civilization in this story. The "Fall of Rome" within the narrative of Western Civilization is exclusively confined to the western section that dissolved in 476 CE.

The construct of Western Civilization is not geographically consistent but considers Greece as the center of civilization in antiquity yet part of the Orient by the nineteenth century. The story of Western Civilization geographically expands and contracts in order to create the desired narrative connections. Given the lack of a fixed geographical boundary, however, there is nothing "natural" about the exclusion of the larger portion of Roman history from the construct.

That the Roman state was an eastern Mediterranean polity for the majority of its history does not fit with the story of the rise of the West. Mathematically speaking, the Roman polity was dominant in the western Mediterranean for roughly seven centuries and in the eastern Mediterranean for either twelve and a half centuries, or sixteen if one counts the Palaiologan recovery.[37] Yet to make Roman history a key step in the story of advancing Western Civilization, the *western* part of Roman history needs to be central to that story. The lopsided temporal predominance of eastern Roman history had to be undercut and discounted.

The primacy of the western part of Roman history was reinforced by emphasizing a sharp break between ancient and modern history in the fifth century,

---

[37] Taking dominance in the West as starting with the conquest of Carthage 202 BC and ending in 476 CE and dominance in the East as starting with the sack of Corinth in 146 BCE and ending in 1204 or 1453 CE.

after which the continued history of the Roman polity was dismissed, often simply through insult. Many versions of the narrative of Western Civilization elevate the collapse of the western Roman Empire into one of the major pivot points of history. The fall of the western empire becomes the break point between ancient and modern history. A popular world history published in 1852 explains this division, stating that "ancient history commences with the Creation, and ends in the year of Christ 476, with the destruction of the Roman Empire in the West. Modern history commences from the fall of that Empire, and extends to the present time."[38] Another echoes: "modern history, in a comprehensive sense, begins with the downfall of the Western Roman empire; for with that event the volume of ancient history was closed: new actors then appeared on the stage, and a new civilization arose."[39]

Since this break was portrayed as cataclysmic and world-altering, the continued existence of new Rome in the East could be glossed over as an anomalous curiosity. The shattering end of western Rome turned the page of history, as it were, to the history of the new "barbarian" kingdoms of the West. Some narratives even omit eastern Rome entirely. One history, inaccurately entitled *History of the Roman Empire, from the Death of Theodosius the Great to the Coronation of Charles the Great, A.D. 395–800*, simply skips from the last western emperor Romulus Augustulus to Charlemagne.[40] One account of world history skips from Alaric to the Latin conquest of Constantinople, and then to the Ottoman conquest with nothing in between.[41]

Another method of skipping over eastern Roman history was to acknowledge its existence but then dismiss it via insult. Histories taking this tack simultaneously attest to the longevity of the eastern empire while declaring it unfit for study. Three of many possible examples include the following:

---

[38] Maunder, *History of the World*, 1:21.

[39] Swinton, *Outlines*, 209. Some historians placed the break between ancient and modern with the advent of Christianity, almost as an expression of piety, but this is much less common. For example: "The event (the birth of Christ) that forms this era, is the most important of events. It has had a commanding influence upon all subsequent history. It has altered the aspect of all human affairs, and it will alter them more and more, as Christianity becomes extended." Robbins, *Outlines*, 2:7.

[40] Curteis, *History of the Roman Empire, from the Death of Theodosius the Great to the Coronation of Charles the Great, A.D. 395–800*, 160.

[41] Maunder, *History of the World*, 296. "We have seen to what a state of degradation the Greeks were reduced in a few centuries after their subjugation by the Romans. Thus it continued as long as it was either really or nominally a portion of the Roman empire; till at length, like the imperial mistress of the world herself, it bent before the all-subduing Alaric the Goth, A.D. 400; and shared in all the miseries which were brought by the northern barbarians who successively overran and ravaged the south of Europe. After the Latin conquest of Constantinople, in 1204, Greece was divided into feudal principalities."

Sailing Away from Byzantium toward East Roman History 17

> While the Roman empire in the West, thus fell into ruins, the sister Empire in the east, which appeared to be in a similar situation, not only continued to stand, but even existed for the space of nearly 1000 years more, though in comparative imbecility and depression.[42]
>
> Byzantine civilization, with its polish and learning and culture on the surface, was petrified and dead at the core, while it was the so-called "barbarous" races of Western Europe that alone held the promise of the future.[43]
>
> The Eastern Empire was not involved in the universal sack, and for a thousand years after the downfall of the Latin Empire, – during which time the new nationalities and the new civilization of Europe were coming into being, – the Eastern, Greek, or Byzantine Empire, as it is called, continued to subsist, though in a state of premature and perpetual decay.[44]

The phrase "in a state of premature and perpetual decay" is Edward Gibbon's. It is a rhetorically powerful zinger of unclear semantic content. What would it mean for a society to subsist in such a state? "Dead at the core" similarly invites dismissal of "Byzantium" rather than a serious consideration of its literal implications. Another textbook has a single paragraph on the eastern empire with a long, unattributed quotation replete with further insults:

> The history of the Byzantine Empire, in the ninth, tenth, and eleventh centuries, is little better than a tissue of usurpation, fanaticism, and perfidy. "Externally surrounded by foes, superior in numbers, in discipline, and in valor, it seemed as if its safety was guaranteed by cowardice, and its security confirmed by defeat. Internally were at work all the causes that usually affect the destruction of states: dishonor and profligacy triumphant in the palace; ferocious bigotry, based at once on enthusiasm and hypocrisy, ruling the church; civil dissensions, equally senseless and bloody, distracting the state; complete demoralization pervading every rank, from the court to the cottage; so that as its existence seemed owing to the antagonizing effect of the causes that singly produce the ruin of empires." In the tenth century these causes seemed to have reached their consummation; Emperor after Emperor were perished by poison, or the dagger of the assassin; parricide and fratricide were crimes of such ordinary occurrence, that they seized to excite feelings of horror or disgust.[45]

This textbook contains exam questions at the back of the book. Usually, the questions pertaining to each section are about the names and dates of key individuals and events. The chapter including "Byzantium," however, takes

---

[42] He continues: "It existed, notwithstanding it suffered all the internal evils which produce the ruin of a state, and was shaken by all the storms, which burst upon the nations, during the Middle Ages. This phenomenon, which is not a parallel in the history of the world, may, in some measure, be explained from the almost impregnable state of its capital alone, in connection with the despotism, which sometimes remains the last support of fallen nations." Robbins, *Outlines*, 2:71.
[43] Swinton, *Outlines*, 219.   [44] Swinton, *Outlines*, 218.
[45] Taylor, *A Manual*, 387. I have not been able to locate the source of the internal quotation.

a different tone. The questions are: (1) "What is said of the history of the Byzantine Empire in the Middle Ages?, and (2) Its condition, etc?" The implication is that the only thing one needed to know about the "Byzantine" Empire was that it was awful.

We shall explore the nature of the insults leveled at eastern Rome in the section on *Teaching Morality and Gender*. Note at this point how they function to separate the history of the corrupt eastern empire from the western part of Roman history, which is valorized. The western Roman state was considered the "real" Rome because it was good, whereas the eastern phase of the polity was characterized by moribund decaying imbecility.

The Age of Faith Is Post-Roman

One of the reasons why a separate "Byzantine" history needed to be detached from Roman history was to enshrine Christianization as a fundamental dividing line in European history. A structural element in the story of Western Civilization is that Europe experienced an Enlightenment and a return to rationality after a medieval Age of Faith. Both those who prized and those who abhorred religion agreed that antiquity was radically different from the Middle Ages, and the crux of that difference was Christianity. Enlightenment intellectuals imagined ancient male elites as secular humanists and decried the descent of the Roman Empire into superstition. The Christianization of the Roman Empire then became the story of the end of the *real* Roman Empire. Christian Roman society necessarily became "Byzantium" because, if its myriad continuities were acknowledged, the notion that Christianity cleanly severed Antiquity from the Middle Age could not be maintained. The fundamental logic of the narrative of Western Civilization – the recovery of rationality and creativity after the Dark Age – required that eastern Roman society cease to exist.

As humanists began to construct an understanding of the "ancient world," separate from the "Dark Ages," the key characteristic of that ancient world was that it was not Christian.[46] For many intellectuals of the sixteenth through eighteenth centuries, the ancient Roman Empire was imagined as a place of rational, enlightened, religious toleration wherein elites occasionally participated in religious rituals as a means of morally correcting superstitious common people without taking those rituals seriously.[47] The image of ancient Roman

---

[46] The idea that the construct of the Byzantine Empire was grounded in European secularism was elaborated by David Turner in an unpublished paper "The Empire Strikes Back: An alternative 'history' of Europe; an Upper House Seminar presented at the British School of Classical Studies in Athens" (1995–6).

[47] Similarly, some Jesuit missionaries in seventeenth-century China considered the intellectual elites whom they admired as truly atheists who only went along with the pagan rituals of their

elite men using religion to control and pacify the masses, while not believing any of it, became a dominant way of understanding Roman religion through much of the twentieth century.[48]

The Christianization of the imperial elite was seen, therefore, as ending a glorious period of religious toleration, and hence a key cause of imperial decline. The change from enlightened secularism to dogmatic religion and intolerance was seen as part of medieval decay. In the words of Montesquieu, "a universal bigotry depressed the courage of the people and stupefied the whole empire."[49] The excessive influence of superstition and clericalism were flaws commonly attributed to "Byzantium." The "exorbitant power of the patriarchs and monks, the fury of theological controversy, the multiplication of schisms and sects" were characteristics that were imputed to "Byzantium" and then blamed for its decline.[50] That Christianity was a key cause of the fall of Rome was accepted in numerous later accounts of Roman history.[51]

The problem with attributing the fall of the Roman Empire to Christianization is that the empire did not end when it became Christian. In order for Gibbon to successfully credit the fall to the twin forces of Barbarism and Religion, he had to kill off the empire in some temporal proximity to the time it became Christian. To do this, he insisted strongly on a division of the eastern and western halves of the polity, claiming priority for the latter. He then deployed masterful rhetoric to define the eastern half as already dead:

> The division of the Roman world between the sons of Theodosius marks the final establishment of the empire of the East, which, from the reign of Arcadius to the taking of Constantinople by the Turks, subsisted one thousand and fifty-eight years, in a state of premature and perpetual decay.[52]

---

society because they were a tool for teaching common people morality. Stroumsa, *A New Science*, 145–57. Nongbri, *Before Religion*, 95. Harvey, "The Rise of Modern Paganism? French Enlightenment Perspectives on Polytheism and the History of Religions," 35.

[48] In Edward Gibbon's eloquent expression: "In their writings and conversation, the philosophers of antiquity asserted the independent dignity of reason; but they resigned their actions to the commands of law and custom. Viewing, with a smile of pity and indulgence, the various errors of the vulgar, they diligently practiced the ceremonies of their fathers, devoutly frequented the temples of the gods; and sometimes condescending to act a part on the theater of superstition, they concealed the sentiments of an Atheist under sacerdotal robes. Reasoners of such a temper were scarcely inclined to wrangle about the respective modes of faith, or of worship." Gibbon, *Decline and Fall*, Chapter 16.

[49] Montesquieu, *Montesquieu's Considerations on the Causes of the Grandeur and Decadence of the Romans*, 448.

[50] Taylor, *A Manual*, 486.

[51] For one example: "The fabric [of the Roman state] naturally tottered to its fall, when the pagan principles of religion, which constituted an essential part of its foundation, were removed." Robbins, *Outlines*, 2:54.

[52] Gibbon, *Decline and Fall*, Chapter 32.

We have already seen that this phrase is as strikingly memorable as it is semantically opaque. Rhetorical finesse thus brilliantly occludes a major logical flaw in his argument. Few readers of Gibbon think to question how Christianity could have killed the empire when half of it was also Christian and did just fine for another millennium. He rather convinces readers that Rome did fall to barbarism and religion in the fifth century, and the eastern half just kept on falling for another ten centuries. Although Gibbon carried his study of the eastern Roman Empire up to the fifteenth century, he succeeded in casting it as entirely different from the "real" Roman Empire in the eyes of generations of readers. Gibbon's narrative rigorously defined Christianity as an aspect of the medieval world and the Roman Empire as, exclusively, part of the ancient world.

The narrative of rupture between a secular antiquity and a religious Middle Ages was also affirmed by people who liked Christianity. Although myriad intellectual and theological positions were taken regarding the merits and demerits of Christianity and paganism during the sixteenth through eighteenth centuries, a general consensus emerged that antiquity was radically different from the Middle Ages, and the crux of that difference was Christianity.[53] It thus became deeply ingrained in European narratives of Western history to see a stark division between ancient and medieval. The continuity of the Roman Empire and the eastern Mediterranean was a fly in the ointment for this vision of history, and so the later empire was excised from Roman history.

One function of the separate label for the "Byzantine" Empire was thus to help cut the Roman Empire into starkly differentiated pagan and Christian halves. Since the true Roman Empire could not be Christian, the establishment of Christianity changed the nature of the polity sufficiently enough to require a change in name. Christianity was thus the essential, definitional element in the historiographic conception of the "Byzantine" Empire.

The conception of the ancient world as nonreligious has been shown to be manifestly false by those scholars working to understand ancient religion without implicit comparison to Christianity. The revisions to our understanding of ancient Roman religion mean that we cannot agree with those Enlightenment scholars who thought the ancient world lacked religion.[54] What reason then is there to see the ancient and medieval empires as separate entities? If the later Empire was labeled "Byzantine," and constructed as a separate object of study,

---

[53] On the variety of thought regarding Christianity in the Enlightenment, see Barnett, *The Enlightenment and Religion*.

[54] A few starting points on a vast field: Scheid, *The Gods, the State, and the Individual*; Champion, *The Peace of the Gods*; Ando, *The Matter of the Gods*; Smith, *Relating Religion*; Smith, *Drudgery Divine*; Beard, North, and Price, *Religions of Rome*.

because it was religious, and we now know that the ancient empire was equally religious, albeit perhaps in different ways, one of the key justifications for separating off a "Byzantine" Empire dissolves. The revisionist research on ancient Roman religion has removed the intellectual cornerstone upon which the "Byzantine" Empire was created.

If Antiquity Isn't Dead, You Can't Renaissance It

Another structural element of the traditional narrative of Western Civilization consists of thinking that western Europeans rediscovered classical antiquity and brought about the Renaissance which put Europe on the path toward the intellectual and cultural greatness that eventually justified European global dominance. The western recovery of a lost antiquity is part of the narrative that valorizes western achievements and establishes the singularity of western excellence. The narrative arc of the Renaissance gives glory to the western European artists and intellectuals who discovered a moribund antiquity. They became pioneers and innovators making wildly new and exciting discoveries in the heritage of antiquity. If one is part of a culture that prizes innovation, novelty, and discovery, these are truly heroic figures.

The truth is that the society and culture of the east Roman Empire continued to be deeply engaged in classical literature, ethics, art, medicine, gender ideals, and philosophy throughout its history. It substantiated much of classical culture in a Christian setting. The existence of this hybrid classical and Christian state, however, throws a monkey wrench into the idea that western European intellectuals "revived" a dormant classical culture in the Renaissance and, more broadly, into the entire schematization of history as having separate classical and medieval periods.

The desire to valorize the western Renaissance required the occlusion and erasure of eastern Roman culture and society from the historical record. Whereas the classicism of Italian artists and authors was lionized as creative engagement with antiquity, the classicism of the eastern Romans was, in the words of Jacob Burckhardt, an "imitation of obsolete motifs." The story examined in the previous section – the fall from an enlightened absence of religion in "antiquity" to a superstitious religiosity in the "medieval" era – worked in tandem with the story of western Renaissance to enforce the break between ancient and medieval ages. As a culture and polity that straddled that divide, eastern Rome needed to be hidden or denied. The rubric of "Byzantium," by allowing the Christian part of the polity to be severed from its origins, made it easier to deny the cultural continuities that would otherwise trouble the Renaissance narrative.

Even when continuity of ancient culture in the East is acknowledged, it is downgraded through negative moral assessments. For example, Robbins' *Outlines of History* explains that those in the "Greek empire" were "a weak or vicious race" whose "degeneracy was rather in moral and intellectual qualities, than in the external show and consequence" as "there remained among them much of ancient wealth and splendor."[55] The continuity of ancient splendor, he suggested, was undercut by their moral weakness.

Even when "Byzantines" are portrayed as possessing ancient literature, there persists an assumption that they were unaffected by its power and virtue. Access to the classical literature of antiquity is frequently portrayed as a springboard to good thought and good taste. One textbook clearly stated: "As the neglect of the standard works of Greece and Rome was one great cause of the decline of learning, and of the bad taste and barbarism of the Middle Ages; so a renewed attention to those works was one great cause of the restoration of learning, taste, and refinement."[56] By this reasoning, the classics were naturally enlightening. Yet in the hands of the "Byzantines," they did not have an impact but were rather a matter of mere external show:

> [the Byzantines] exhibited all the externals of advanced civilization. They possessed knowledge; they had continually before them the noble literature of ancient Greece, instinct with the loftiest heroism; but that literature, which afterwards did so much to revivify Europe, could fire the degenerate Greeks with no spark or semblance of nobility.[57]

Their possession of learning was not credited as a useful employment of classical literature. They were apparently immune to its salutary effects. Accusations of degeneracy and dullness form the only explanations given for the imputed inefficacy of classical literature. This narrative of "Byzantine" immunity to the impact of classical literature is highly useful in that it keeps "true" engagement with classics as a matter of purely Western history.

To make western Hellenists into autonomous innovators, rather than students of foreigners, eastern Roman traditions of classicism had to be negated. Eastern Roman classicism is often denied simply through insult. The charge is routinely made that eastern Roman philologists copied texts without understanding them. "Byzantine" scholars are credited with "preserving" classics, but not using them. They are cast as necessary idiots: "Pedantic, dull, blundering as they are too often, they are indispensable."[58] The very lack of engagement attributed to "Byzantine" scholars is then interpreted as a positive characteristic in that

---

[55] Robbins, *Outlines*, 1:119.   [56] Robbins, *Outlines*, 2:389.
[57] Lecky, *History of European Morals*, 13.   [58] Harrison, *Byzantine History*, 36.

they preserved the classics for more insightful peoples. In an essay attempting to *rehabilitate* the reputation of "Byzantium," Frederic Harrison explained:

> We pick precious truths and knowledge out of their garrulities and stupidities, for they preserve what otherwise would have been lost forever. It is no paradox that their very merit to us is that they were never either original or brilliant. Their genius indeed would have been our loss. Dunces and pendants as they were, they servilely repeated the words of the immortals. Had they not done so, the immortals would have died long ago.[59]

Logically, this line of thought would indicate that each publication of a critical edition is an act of servile repetition. The "Byzantines" were considered to have lacked creativity. They could be credited with scholarship, but not originality.[60]

This evaluation hinges on the ability of the modern scholar to distinguish a creative classical allusion to an ancient text from a repetitive or imitative "Byzantine" classical allusion. At an epistemological level, how would the early modern and modern writers, denigrating "Byzantines" for "mindless repetition," know what was going on inside the mind of the medieval Roman person? This is in every case a baseless accusation beyond proof. If it had been presented as hypothesis for exploration, it would have been resoundingly refuted by the abundant evidence that medieval eastern Romans were thoughtful in their classicism and used their classical knowledge creatively. On the contrary, the accusation of mindlessness operates most often at the level of base name-calling: "much of the art was lifeless and all the literature jejune."[61] The shudder-inducing horror at eastern Roman classicism became something of an in-joke among western classicists upholding the exclusivity of their own fancy educations. According to this reasoning, western intellectuals playing with classical texts are creative, whereas eastern intellectuals were repetitive.

The Roman Empire that was conquered by crusaders in the thirteenth century was a Homer-quoting, Aristotle-reading, ancient history-writing society deeply in touch with its classical heritage. Until the discovery of papyrus fragments, all of the surviving texts from classical Greek antiquity were preserved by eastern Romans because they were prized in that culture. It was not accidental. They were selected, recopied, commented upon, studied in schools, riffed on in rhetoric competitions, and formed part of the most basic cultural background knowledge in east Roman society. The allusions to classical texts in eastern Roman cultural products are pervasive. They did indeed think about what they were reading and copying, not only quoting ancient texts, but making far more

---

[59] Harrison, *Byzantine History*, 36–37.
[60] "The intellectual history of later Greece was a different character from that of its glorious period. There was more of scholarship, but less of creative genius." Swinton, *Outlines*, 109.
[61] Harrison, *Byzantine History*, 15.

subtle unattributed intertextual allusions, that relied on the assumption that their audiences would know Plutarch, for example, well enough to complete the meaning of the allusion without prompting.[62]

The function of the accusation of thoughtless repetitions is clear: It turns the later Romans into a preservative gel that kept the classics pure and unadulterated for the later use of the West. The "Byzantines," in their undead state of premature and perpetual decay, worked like formaldehyde. This was a necessary step for the Renaissance narrative to work. If antiquity was not dead, the West could not give it its rebirth. Again, the functionally dead and zombie-state of "Byzantium" was necessary to get later Roman culture and society out of the way of the narrative of Western Civilization.

Teaching Morality and Gender

Another function of "Byzantium" was as morality play that exhorted western Europeans, and European-descended Americans, to proper behavior. Throughout the eighteenth and nineteenth centuries, writers decried "Byzantine" morals, religion, and lack of progress. Remarkably, for a polity that they considered to have lasted for 1,058 years, the discussion always centered on the decline, perhaps because the state was seen as existing in "premature and perpetual decay."

In the nineteenth century, moral decay was commonly understood as the cause of the decline of nations. As one short essay, reprinted numerous times in a variety of newspapers and collections, put it:

> Why do nations die? Cultivated Greece, and all-conquering Rome; Vandal, and Goth, and Hun, and Moor, and Pole, and Turk, all dead or dying. Why? Murdered by nations more powerful? Swallowed by earthquakes? Swept away by pestilence or plague, or starved by pitiless famine? Not by any of these. ... They perished by moral degradation, the legitimate result of gluttony, intemperance and effeminacy.

The clear lesson for the audience is that "each man owes it to himself, to his country, and, more than all, to his Maker, to live a life of temperance, industry and self-denial as to every animal gratification; and with these having an eye to the glory of God, this nation of ours will live with increasing prosperity and renown."[63] The fall of the western empire was a favorite case used to make this moral point. A textbook from 1837 concluded emphatically:

---

[62] On one of myriad possible examples, Neville, "Singing with David and Contemplating Agesilaus," 140–58. Fundamental guidance: Papaioannou, ed., *The Oxford Handbook of Byzantine Literature*.
[63] "Dying Nations," *Hall's Journal of Health*; "Read, Read! Read!!" *Boston Investigator*; "Dying Nations," *Vermont Journal*; "Dying Nations," *Connersville Examiner*; "Dying Nations," in *The Christian Treasury*, 18:83; "Dying Nations," *Herald of Gospel Liberty*; "Dying Nations," *The*

> The ruin of the Roman Empire, was the result of its great extent, connected with its moral corruption. ... Rome, having become a mass of luxury, weakness, and profligacy, fell, at last, an easy prey to the barbarous tribes that poured in upon its dominions.[64]

This exhortation to moral temperance appeals to history without making an argument based on particular events. The connection between moral decay and decline is asserted and regarded as axiomatic rather than argued.

The logical difficulty with this argument is that the lurid stories of moral corruption, which ultimately derive from Tacitus and the *Historia Augustae*, do not chronologically overlap with periods of economic or military difficulties. Linking the "crimes" of Elagabalus in 220 with the sack of Rome in 410 is like blaming the 2016 US election on the moral turpitude of John Quincy Adams in 1826. The moral argument was made much more vaguely: moral corruption, in general, led to decline. The dearly loved connection between moral decay and decline of nations is in fact extraordinarily difficult to substantiate with historical details because sex, booze, and greed seem to be distributed fairly evenly throughout history. Societies containing groups that are deeply committed to rooting out vice tend to produce a lot of literature talking about that vice. Powerful elites are criticized for their excessive luxury whenever they get wealthy enough to have luxury. While inept choices by powerful leaders do have a disproportionately significant impact on societies, it is nearly impossible to pin specific moments of failure to levels of vice that existed at that particular moment and not others.

The construction of the "Byzantine" polity helped ease this fundamental difficulty with the moral decline argument because it was defined as a society that was *always* in decline. Any moral problems attributed to "Byzantium" could be immediately connected with political decay because it was conceived of as a society perpetually falling. All of the moral problems that were imputed to it were taken as evidence of the connection between moral decay and decline. Since the realities of later Roman history needed to be occluded anyway, this zombie polity could be made to represent whatever worries later writers had. The desire to make history a useful compendium of moral lessons fueled the tradition of extravagantly denouncing the evils of the "Byzantines" in often lurid and overwrought detail.

This corrupt Empire tradition additionally became a way for authors to articulate values that a proper upstanding progressive European man would

---

Co-Operative News and Journal of Associated Industry; "Dying Nations," *Georgetown Courier*. Quoted completely in Thompson, *Nineteen Christian Centuries in Outline*, 152.

[64] This author attributes the fall to divine punishment for "enormously guilty nations." Robbins, *Outlines*, 2:71.

not have. The discussion of what was wrong with "Byzantium" is interwoven at every turn with conceptions of proper behavior for western European and North American men. The following are typical examples of the corrupt Empire discourse:

> The Byzantine empire displays a melancholy picture of moral depravity. A court filled with oriental luxury and magnificence, where women and favourites raise and dethrone weak or vicious emperors by crimes or intrigues; an insolent body-guard, who carried on the same audacious game with the crown that the pretorians had formerly done; and a fickle population, who took pleasure in nothing but questions of religious controversy, and the rude sports of the race-course.[65]
>
> Of that Byzantine Empire the universal verdict of history is that it constitutes, with scarcely an exception, the most thoroughly base and despicable form that civilization has yet assumed. Though very cruel and very sensual, there have been times when cruelty assumed more ruthless, and sensuality more extravagant aspects; but there has been no other enduring civilization so absolutely destitute of all the forms and elements of greatness, and known to which the epithet *mean* may be so emphatically implied.[66]

These descriptions seem intended to spark a feeling of revulsion among the readers. The sensationalized vocabulary steps out of normal modes of historical description and builds florid rants against the horrors of "Byzantium."

While most scholars of later Rome are familiar with these anti-Byzantine screeds, we dismiss them more often than we have considered the nature of the complaints. Gender, and more specifically misogyny, lies either on the surface or in the background of many of the imputed failings of "Byzantium." In the rest of this section, I will unpack some of the values and desires expressed through the virulent critiques of "Byzantium" and explicate the ways in which I see these complaints as cumulatively casting "Byzantium" as an evil woman.

A prevalent characteristic attributed to the "Byzantines" was their degeneracy. In ancient days, according to the corrupt Empire discourse, the Greeks had been absolutely admirable, but somehow they lost their greatness and became objects of revulsion. It was not uncommon to accuse the Greeks of losing their luster. This fall from greatness was a fascinating horror story told time and again as part of the project warning western Europeans to be careful with their moral status. The "Byzantines" proved that a great people could go bad, and hence struck terror into the hearts of all those trying to be great.

A first phase of the degeneration of the Greeks is often attributed to the time of their conquest by the Romans, with additional declines placed during the fall of the western empire. According to Samuel Maunder's history, after the Roman

---

[65] Weber, *Outlines*, 125.   [66] Lecky, *History of European Morals*, 13.

conquest of Greece: "The character of the nation was now sunk so low the nation scarcely showed a trace of the noble characteristics of their fathers."[67] Further degeneration is attributed to the fifth and sixth centuries.[68] This was when "the people sank into a nation of pedants, parasites, and adventurers."[69] These descriptions of "Byzantine degeneracy" work within a system of thought in which nations were expected to have different defining characteristics. The prospect that a "great nation" like the ancient Greeks could become an ignoble nation served as a warning.

Discussions of the degeneracy or rise of various nations are sometimes interwoven with more overtly racial theories of decline. In much nineteenth-century historical writing, the battles over racial continuity and replacement took place alongside discourses of racial improvement and decline. William Swinton, the writer of a popular general history, described races as both structural entities[70] and as subject to change, with significant consequences, ultimately blaming the fall of (western) Roman Empire on racial mixture:

> [T]he Roman *race*, which conquered the world, was finally swallowed up by the world which it conquered. The blood itself was corrupted by alien admixture.[71]

This overt blaming of the decline of the Romans on miscegenation is not typical, but the ubiquitous descriptions of the "Byzantines" as having degenerated from the Romans laid the groundwork for Swinton's racialization of the process of decline.

Descriptions of Roman decline can be highly sexualized as well as racialized. Consider the description in Maunder's 1852 *History of the World:*

> The individual hardihood and pride of manhood that characterized the Roman of the Republic, and the serried discipline and national pride that had so often given prey to the Roman Eagle, under the Roman emperors who were worthy of that name, had passed away before a luxury and effeminacy which would be incredible were they not related to us by the pens of indignant Romans. . . . But enough has been said to show that the state of Rome, alike in government and people, was precisely such as to invite, nay, to require, the rude purification of successive and successful invasions of hardier races. Alaric again and again ravaged the Roman territories, Honorius and his ministers literally inviting him to do so by their pusillanimity on some occasions and empty threats on others.[72]

---

[67] Maunder, *History of the World*, 2:294.
[68] "After the death of Theodosius, all degenerated; and from this epoch may be dated the fall of the Romans." Maunder, *History of the World*, 2:277.
[69] Swinton, *Outlines*, 109.
[70] "The historical races of Europe comprise four grand divisions of the great Aryan stock, – the Graeco-Latins, the Celts, the Teutons, and the Slavs, or Slavonians," Swinton, *Outlines*, 210.
[71] Swinton, *Outlines*, 204. Emphasis in the original.   [72] Maunder, *History of the World*, 2:45.

The description of the old victorious Romans and the fifth-century conquerors with the terms "hardihood" and "hardier," contrasted with the "effeminacy" of the later Romans, presents the act of conquest with a terminology that brings to mind sexualized masculine aggression. The "luxury and effeminacy" of the later Romans sets them as feminine victims of rape, "again and again ravaged" by Alaric. The later Romans are described as desiring this "rude purification" which they are said, twice, to have invited. They become not only women, but lustful women, as the cause of their metaphorical rape is placed on them rather than the masculine conquerors. Although we can safely assume that not all nineteenth-century readers consciously picked up on the highly sexualized nature of this description, the implicit demasculinization of the later Romans is inescapable. Part of the story of the degeneration of the Romans was from the "hardihood" of their martial, masculine, discipline to the luxurious effeminacy that begged to be ravaged. The Romans morphed from exemplary men to deplorable women.

Religion

Poor religious practices of the "Byzantines" were another topic of complaint. For Jean-Baptiste de Rocoles, writing in the reign of Louis XIV, piety meant being Catholic, and the lesson of his chapter on the "Impiety and Wickedness" of the "Byzantine" emperors was that good rulers should be Catholic and moral. The problems of the "Byzantine" emperors were their "cruelty, avarice, perfidy and ... ingratitude," but most of all their lack of communion with the Catholic church.[73] Other writers criticized icon veneration, devotion to saints, and aspects of "Byzantine" religion that were unlike Protestantism.

These complaints about incorrect theology and practice, however, are dwarfed by the accusation that the "Byzantines" were simply too religious and fanatical. "Superstition" was one of the chief failings of the "Byzantines." They fell into "paroxysms of religious agitation"[74] that distracted from serious matters. They had disproportionately fanatical responses to small points of theology: "[T]he people only emerged from their listlessness when some theological subtlety, or some rivalry in the chariot races, stimulated them into frantic riots."[75] Religious controversy was cast as a dangerous preoccupation: "Whilst the provinces were thus falling, one after another, into the hands of the

---

[73] "The vices of the most part of the emperors were the principle cause of the destruction of their empire. Without speaking of their atrocious crimes, their cruelty, avarice, perfidy and their ingratitude, which made their memory an eternal execration, we find barely 20 of 90 who followed Orthodox doctrine and who had submitted to the church." Rocoles, *Introduction Generale a l'histoire Prophane: Contenant Son Parfait Usage*, 2:238.

[74] Lecky, *History of European Morals*, 13.   [75] Lecky, *History of European Morals*, 13.

neighboring powers, the empire itself was convulsed by the disputes of political and religious parties."[76] A lamentable decline of "patriotism and public spirit" was attributed to this excessive religiosity.[77] They could not develop new policies because they were "clinging superstitiously to antiquated formulas."[78]

The discourse of "Byzantine superstition" is markedly gendered with associations between excessive religiosity and negative stereotypes about women, coding "Byzantine" society as negatively feminine. The complaint that "luxury, effeminacy, and superstition sapped its vitals"[79] bundles superstition with vices of being too much like women. "Byzantine" religion was seen as undermining the capacity for rational thought and action among the population. Both rational thought and action were treated as masculine traits, whereas gullibility and simpleminded faith were considered feminine traits. A society that substituted superstition for rational thought was implicitly an unthinking feminized society. Insofar as the frenzied, emotional, implicitly feminized behaviors intruded into politics, "Byzantine superstition" was a feminization of the public sphere.

The influence of women is sometimes overtly named as a cause of increasing superstition. Finlay lamented that a supposed increase in women's control over family education improved morals, but "certainly increased superstition and limited men's understandings." As "family education" increased at the expense of "public instruction," "nurses and slaves implanted their ignorant superstitions in the households where the rulers of the empire and the provinces were reared."[80] This connection between women, education, and superstition makes silly religion a specifically feminine problem.

Within this discourse, men could certainly be superstitious, but when they did, they were acting like women. The increase in superstition seen in "Byzantine" society was not overtly stated as a problem of feminization, but clearly it added to the conception of "Byzantium" as a bad society because it was not manly. The genre of corrupt Empire screeds upholds ancient ideas of masculine rationality and feminine gullibility.

Backward Conservatism

"Byzantine" society was characterized as opposed to progress, which in the minds of many nineteenth-century thinkers amounted to a grave failing. Finlay flatly declared that "the Byzantine Greeks always rejected the idea of progress."[81] Eastern conservatism, from this standpoint, becomes a foil that

---

[76] Pütz, *Handbook*, 32.   [77] Swinton, *Outlines*, 109.   [78] Finlay, *History*, 3:280.
[79] Maunder, *History of the World*, 1:45.   [80] Finlay, *History*, 2:4–5.
[81] Finlay, *History*, 3:280.

highlights a peculiarly upward trajectory of Western society. Constructing the East as backward-looking was a way to dismiss it while lauding the West. As Swinton put it: "[W]e shall not be greatly concerned with the affairs of the Eastern Empire, because progress lay not there, but in the West."[82]

Although the West after the fall of the western empire was considered to have been in a state of barbarism, it was nonetheless on the way up. Western European kingdoms were "already emerging from their social degradation" and were indicating "paths of reform" that the "Byzantines" lamentably did not follow.[83] "Byzantine" conservatism helped code the West as rising and the East as declining. As Finley put it: "[W]hile the rest of Europe was actively striving to attain a happier future, the Greeks were gazing backward on what they considered a more glorious past."[84] One textbook explained the comparison of the West and the East as "from a scene of vivid if rude and barbarous energy, to a life better ordered, yet on the whole less noble."[85] In Harrison's attempt at a positive portrayal of "Byzantium," the contrast remains one of growth versus stasis:

> Western Europe, no doubt, bore within its bosom the seeds of a far greater world to come, a more virile youth, greater heroes and chiefs. But wealth, organization, knowledge, for the time were safeguarded behind the walls of Byzantium.[86]

It is not difficult to notice the implied masculine activity of the virility and vivid energy of the western barbarian states in contrast to the feminine passivity and domesticity of safeguarding behind walls. The West actively strives for the future while the East passively gazes backward.

Proponents of progress decried the lack of whiggish government among the "Byzantines." Finley calls out the medieval empire for failing to invest in infrastructure:

> [T]he funds appropriated in preceding times to uphold the most indispensable adjuncts of civilization were either annihilated or diverted from their destination. Ports, bridges, roads, aqueducts, and fortifications were falling to ruin in every province. Court spectacles and ecclesiastical ceremonies at the capital absorbed the funds which had been accumulated in distant municipalities for local improvements, hospitals, and schools.[87]

He left out the railroads. Finley argued that this lack of investment sapped the zeal for national independence.[88] These complaints encode constant progress as

---

[82] Swinton, *Outlines*, 219. [83] Finley, *History*, 3:280. [84] Finley, *History*, 3:280.
[85] Curteis, *History of the Roman Empire, from the Death of Theodosius the Great to the Coronation of Charles the Great, A.D. 395–800*, 172.
[86] Harrison, *Byzantine History*, 12. [87] Finley, *History*, 3:219–20.
[88] "Everything that could inspire the people with zeal to defend their national independence had disappeared, or was rapidly disappearing. Political despotism, national demoralization, ecclesiastical

a fundamental aspect of a successful society and act as a manifesto for what a good government ought to provide.

The contrast of western progress to eastern backwardness and conservatism is a contrast between activity and passivity, and hence also comes with gendered implications. The contrast between a vigorous virile society enacting reforms and striving for progress and a static conservative society characterized as "superstitiously repeating antiquated formulas" is between one coded as positively masculine and the other as negatively feminine.

The imputed lack of interest in progress became a trope that reinforced the belief that "Byzantine" culture was not inventive or creative. "Byzantine" "literature lost its vigor; arts deteriorated."[89] This society was "without a genius or intellectual activity."[90] The imputed lack of creativity combined with the trope of servility, which will be discussed in the following section, to reinforce the idea of that "Byzantine" scholars mindlessly repeated past ideas. The attribution of a lack of progressive spirit to the "Byzantines" reinforced the story that their scholarship was a matter of stale repetition. "Byzantine" conservatism was one of the reasons that the classicism of the European Renaissance was considered fundamentally different.

This image of the servilely repetitive "Byzantine" pedants is of a negatively feminized form of scholarship. It allows that the later Roman classicists had skill but not creativity. Like feminine craft, they repeated fossilized forms, rather than masculine art. The art of the West was characterized as free and contrasted with the fossilized repetition of "Byzantinism."[91] The implicit negative feminization of later Roman scholars and artists helped uphold the idea that "Byzantium" played wetnurse for Renaissance man. In an overt expression of a frequently implied idea, Harrison explained:

> It is impossible to see how our knowledge of ancient literature or civilization could have been recovered if Constantinople had not nursed through the early Middle Ages the vast accumulations of Greek learning.[92]

"Byzantium," in his telling, was the feminine nurse who tended the precious ancient learning; the vessel in which ancient civilization gestated silently and passively until birthed by the western Renaissance Man. In casting the eastern Roman classicists as dunces and pedants, and as implicitly feminized nurses,

---

corruption, fiscal oppression, and habitual misgovernment, must therefore be considered responsible for the anarchical and disorderly state of Constantinople at the accession of Isaac Angelos." Finlay, *History*, 3:219–20.

[89] Swinton, *Outlines*, 109. [90] Lecky, *History of European Morals*, 13.

[91] Milman, *History of Latin Christianity; Including That of the Popes to the Pontificate of Nicolas V*., 8:476.

[92] Harrison, *Byzantine History*, 36. Emphasis mine.

this discourse insults both those scholars *and* women more generally. Using imputed feminization of the passive "Byzantine" scholars to denigrate that culture simultaneously reinforced misogyny.

Free West and Servile East

The supposed submissiveness of the "Byzantines" is another strand of the corrupt Empire discourse that focuses on problems ascribed to the East: Oriental servility and luxury. Within the context of this discourse, the complaints of servility and luxury help to construct a contrasting image of western culture as freedom-loving, vigorous, and overwhelmingly masculine.

A significant aspect in the degradation of the glorious ancient Greeks to "Byzantines" was the loss of their thirst for freedom and the growth of their servility. Some typical complaints are expressed as follows:

> The Oriental habits of servility and adulation superseded the old free-spoken independence and manliness ...[93]
> ... their ancient love of freedom and independence was extinguished; and a mean servility was substituted in its place.[94]
> Without patriotism, without the fruition or desire of liberty, ... slaves, and willing slaves, in both their actions and their thoughts immersed in sensuality and in the most frivolous pleasures.[95]

Even in these few examples we can see that freedom is associated with manliness and servility with the feminine-coded traits of sensuality and frivolity. Servility is aligned with both passive femininity and being Eastern. "Oriental" despotism supposedly instilled slavish behavior in the servile "Byzantines," who were docile and submissive like women rather than standing up for themselves like real men.

Another aspect of the degradation of the Greeks from their ancient glory was imputed to the corruption of eastern luxury. After the conquests of Alexander the Great, "there was a reflex influence of Asia on the Hellas herself."[96] A consequence was that "Asiatic luxury had wholly corrupted them."[97] This decadence of the Greeks, ascribed to the Hellenistic and early Roman eras, continued to be seen as an integral part of "Byzantine" society. As an "Oriental" society, "Byzantium" was considered prone to luxury, softness, and sexual indulgence. This well-known discourse connected the East with effeminacy and called on Europeans to resist the allure of the exotic, luxurious Orient by

---

[93] Swinton, *Outlines*, 109.   [94] Maunder, *History of the World*, 2:294.
[95] Lecky, *History of European Morals*, 13.   [96] Swinton, *Outlines*, 109.
[97] Maunder, *History of the World*, 2:294.

exercising rational domination.[98] Excessive luxury was a corrupting problem described as a cause of the decline of the western Romans.[99]

Sometimes "Byzantium" is quite overtly described as feminized, as in "luxury, effeminacy, and superstition sapped its vitals."[100] At other times, the association is implied or simply one of proximity. Voltaire's frequently quoted judgment that the "history of Byzantium" was "a disgrace to the human mind, as the Greek empire was a disgrace to the world," is given, not in the main body of any of his writings, but in a footnote occasioned by his discussion of the deviant sexual practices of Elagabalus. Voltaire says that Elagabalus had himself circumcised to enjoy sexual pleasure with women, and then castrated to have more with men.[101] This story prompts the footnote decrying "the history of Byzantium" as even more ridiculous. Voltaire is ostensibly making the point that these stories do not merit belief, and that the "Byzantine" histories contain nothing but "speeches and miracles." Yet the context of the discussion of Elagabalus' supposed voluntary eunuchism associates the ridiculousness of "Byzantine" history with both sexual deviance and effeminacy.

Powerful Women

"Byzantium" was further feminized and demonized through association with overly powerful women. The power held by "priests, eunuchs, and women" constituted a gender inversion that seemingly left European readers shuddering in disgust.[102] The sway of women over their emperors was depicted as a failing of the latter's masculine self-determination. Moreover, they influenced men in bad ways. Arcadius "suffered himself to be governed by favorites, and at length by Eudoxia, his empress, who made it her great object to plunder the revenues of the state."[103] Here he failed by allowing Eudoxia to govern him, especially since her object was to harm the polity. Otherwise, good emperors were depicted as undermined by the influence of their wives. Justinian, for example, "was a pious and diligent sovereign, ... he would have surpassed Augustus, but

---

[98] "Byzantium was constructed as the decadent, effeminate foil to a vigorous, manly Europe: In short, as an especially proximate branch of an imagined Orient." Anderson and Ivanova, eds., *Is Byzantine Studies a Colonialist Discipline?: Toward a Critical Historiography*, 3. Marciniak, "Oriental Like Byzantium."

[99] Reference to "the effeminate and luxurious matters of the nobles and people of Rome" in Maunder, *History of the World*, 2:277. See also "luxury further demoralized the people" in Swinton, *Outlines*, 204.

[100] Maunder, *History of the World*, 1:45.

[101] Voltaire, *Œuvres Complètes de Voltaire Avec Des Remarques et Des Notes Historiques, Scientifiques et Littéraires: Par MM. Auquis, Clogenson, ... et al.*, 97 v., 369.

[102] Lecky, *History of European Morals*, 13.   [103] Robbins, *Outlines*, 2:66.

he yielded his power to the infamous Theodora, and to unworthy ministers who abused his confidence, and oppressed the empire."[104] Another scholar called Theodora's influence "exceedingly injurious to the interests of the empire."[105] What specifically Theodora had done to the empire was not specified; the existence of female influence was itself seen as bad.

Powerful women are overrepresented in descriptions of "Byzantium." Both of the textbooks cited in the previous paragraph as decrying Theodora's influence cover history at a high altitude, only mentioning the most remarkably politically influential individuals. Theodora was simply not important enough to merit mention in these broad histories, were it not for a particular interest in pointing out the pernicious effects of female power. Similarly, a disproportionate amount of space in Robbins' history is given to empress Eirene (797–803), whom he calls "a monster of wickedness" and "singularly cruel."[106]

Women indeed were able to influence high-level politics and serve as regents in all eras of the Roman Empire. Women reigned, briefly, without male colleagues in the eighth and eleventh centuries. European attention to these powerful women is disproportionate to the effects of their authority – they did not rule any differently than the many civilian male emperors. No particular policies or unusual actions can be attributed to the gender of these female rulers. Catholic historians have at times upheld the piety of Eirene and the ninth-century regent Theodora because of their role in ending iconoclasm, while Protestant historians blamed the downfall of iconoclasm on their addled female superstition. In both cases, however, these rulers were behaving perfectly normally in calling church councils to establish the theological stance they thought was best for the empire.

Given the absence of any unusual patterns in the political authority of women rulers, the critique of their presence in positions of power is grounded entirely in their gender. The "Byzantine" Empire was criticized for the power of empresses apparently because women simply ought not have power over men. Women's influence was also portrayed as harmful. The associations of women with luxury, frivolity, and superstition led naturally to assumptions that their influence would be injurious to the interests of the state.

The imputed problem of women in power was closely linked with criticism of "Byzantine" politics. The corrupt Empire discourse fulminated thunderously against the intrigue and treachery of the "Byzantine" court. Yet the essential

---

[104] Taylor, *A Manual*, 334.
[105] Pütz, *Handbook*, 30. "Theodora, the wife of this emperor, a woman of debauched character, who had formerly been an actress, exercised an influence which her profligate and cruel disposition rendered exceedingly injurious to the interests of the empire."
[106] Robbins, *Outlines*, 2:90.

negative feminization of "Byzantine intrigue" has not been sufficiently appreciated. On the one hand, wickedness, cruelty, licentiousness, and profligacy were attributed to individual empresses. At a more subtle level, the extreme distaste expressed for "Byzantine" court politics seems to reflect the relative absence of straightforwardly agonistic male combat. Here are some typical descriptions of "Byzantine" politics:

> Successive emperors were hurled from the throne, deprived of sight, maimed, shut up in convents, or put to death, sometimes through the intrigues of ambitious consorts and their paramours, sometimes by their own sons, their ministers, or the victorious generals of their armies.[107]
>
> Wicked princes ascended the blood-stained throne in the midst of the most revolting horrors; deprivation of the eyes, mutilation of the nose and ears, were things of daily occurrence in this God-forsaken court.[108]
>
> The history of the Empire is a monotonous story of the intrigues of priests, eunuchs, and women, of poisonings, of conspiracies, of uniform ingratitude, of perpetual fratricides.[109]
>
> Emperor after Emperor perished by poison, or the dagger of the assassin; parricide and fratricide were crimes of such ordinary occurrence, that they ceased to excite feelings of horror or disgust.[110]

What motivates the rich revulsion of these descriptions? As with the criticism of women in power, they are, in a sense, a response to aspects of Roman political practice. The bloodstained throne is a metaphor arising from the nature of Roman political succession. Since Julius Caesar adopted Octavian as his heir, the mechanism for imperial succession in the Roman Empire was a mixture of familial descent, adoption, fictive kinship, deposition, proclamation, and revolt.[111] Emperors ruled for as long as enough of the right people thought they were doing a decent job, and few enjoyed a post-deposition retirement. Outright civil warfare between contending emperors was relatively rare, confined mostly to periods of crisis in the middle of the third century and the five decades following Diocletian's attempt to regularize succession through the tetrarchy. No wars between sons of emperors were fought after the fourth century. Those who were proclaimed emperor by armies or court factions either succeeded in becoming the next emperor or had their revolts squashed. This system meant that being emperor, or the member of an imperial family, was dangerous business. The average length of a reign was ten years and simple succession from father to son was hardly the norm. It was, however,

---

[107] Pütz, *Handbook*, 32.   [108] Weber, *Outlines*, 127.
[109] Lecky, *History of European Morals*, 13.   [110] Taylor, *A Manual*, 387.
[111] Rocoles, an early commentator on "Byzantium," was astounded at the non-hereditary nature of Byzantine succession. Rocoles, *Introduction Generale a l'histoire Prophane: Contenant Son Parfait Usage*, 2:235, 257.

a remarkably stable system in that this polity lasted for 1,241 years (1,490 years if one includes the Palaiologan restoration). This makes it among the most successful political systems in written human history.

Given that it worked so well, we need to explore why this system filled European observers with such horror. The blood spilled in the system of Roman imperial succession was generally localized within the imperial family. Emperors were deposed through murder. Sons and other male relatives sometimes joined their fate or were blinded and tonsured as monks. Murder and mutilation were indeed aspects of Roman imperial succession. In a gallon for gallon comparison of blood spilt, however, it is abundantly clear that Roman systems for promoting and demoting emperors were far more peaceable than contemporaneous western European dynastic politics. Troublesome succession disputes in western European medieval kingdoms were solved by having the contestants gather armies, meet on a field, and battle it out. The size and viciousness of these military conflicts varied with the scale of the kingdoms involved, but all included physical casualties among combatants, economic destruction of surrounding communities, and mass civilian death. Comparing the destructiveness and loss of life common in this sort of dynastic violence with one man getting drowned in a bathtub, the rational conclusion ought to be that the Roman political system was remarkably *un*-bloody.

At heart, the problem with "Byzantine" politics was that, in limiting the opportunities for straightforward field combat between men, it was feminized. That eastern emperors were disposed of quickly with a single knife rather than surrounded by scorched fields and dozens of loyal, dead warriors is taken not as a sign of peacefulness but of moral corruption.

Eastern politics were routinely described as palace "intrigue," a word used for scheming women in back rooms. Within a cultural system that kept women out of the public sphere, women engaged in politics almost exclusively within the domestic sphere of their imperial households, out of the public eye. Their political activity hence always counted as "intrigue" rather than public deliberation or warfare. Eunuchs, civilian bureaucrats, and purposefully demilitarized male members of the imperial household all also engaged in politics within the ambiguously domestic space of the palace, and hence they too engaged in "intrigue." Any political activity by Roman women, from Livia on, could be classified as such.[112] In allowing the occasional participation of women and eunuchs, this system was seen as feminized. The horror expressed at the

---

[112] One example of many: Voltaire calls Julia Domna and Julia Maesa "intrigantes": Voltaire, *Œuvres Complètes de Voltaire avec des remarques et des notes historiques, scientifiques et littéraires: Par MM. Auquis, Clogenson, ... et al.*, 369.

imputed cruelty and intrigue of the "Byzantine" court is hence grounded in misogyny.

The criticism of the civilian politics of "Byzantium" in the corrupt Empire discourse works to valorize the militarized politics of the medieval west. A whole constellation of male virtues – hierarchical loyalty, straightforward honesty, strength, and fighting prowess – could be upheld as valuable through vilifying the supposedly contrasting, explicitly feminized, "Byzantine intrigue." The preferred politics became that of the battles between the kings of Wessex and Mercia in which the most effective military combatant won. Masculine strength was devalued in "Byzantine" politics where a big, strong man did not always have a distinct advantage over women and eunuchs. This system nullified the advantages of brawn by not deciding all conflicts "on the field" in open confrontations in which men face off and see who was left standing. Hence "Byzantine" politics was considered both feminized and emasculating.

Functions of the Corrupt Empire Discourse

The primary work of the corrupt Empire discourse was to sever the awful "Byzantine" Empire from the wonderful western empire. Constructing "Byzantium" as degenerate, servile, superstitious, and feminine, reinforced its cleavage from the valorized classical Roman Empire and allowed western Europe to be the only heirs of the later. Casting "Byzantines" as feminized imbeciles severed them from the *real* Romans so that Roman heritage became the exclusive patrimony of properly dominant men like Charlemagne and the builders of various European empires.

The degeneration of the Romans from strong, masculine conquerors to soft, decadent victims of conquest also provided a riveting cautionary tale that has persistently haunted European imaginations. The frightful "Byzantinization" of the Roman Empire has been a constant reminder that the danger of descent into feminizing luxury and despotism is always just a few missteps away. Whereas the classical Roman Empire served as a model for later Europeans of what a "good" empire could be, the "Byzantine Empire" became a frightening model of how bad things could get. "Byzantium" has provided one of the most consistent ideological motivators in European history.

The misogynistic thread running throughout the corrupt Empire discourse makes feminization the flaw most greatly to be feared. The critiques of the "Byzantine Empire" as effeminate, servile, Oriental, superstitious, decadent, uncreative, and luxuriant are, at their core, motivated by the fear of poorly performed gender. The underlying problem Europeans projected onto the

"Byzantines" was that they were not "proper" men. The feminization of the "Byzantine" Empire served as a warning to western European readers to avoid those problems. The contrast with a feminized "Byzantium" helped reinforce ideals of Western masculinity. Western men were portrayed as creative, rational, moderate, progressive, straightforward, and worthy fighters on the field. They were free from the influence of women in religion, education, or politics. In successfully ignoring women they upheld a heteronormative hierarchy.

The discourse of "Byzantium" not only defines the East as feminine and the West as masculine, but femininity as *bad*. The contrast is between a good masculine rationality and bad feminine superstition, between good masculine creativity and bad feminine copying, good dominating masculinity and bad passive and slavish femininity, good head-on masculine combat, and bad feminine intrigue. This discourse does as much to define women negatively as it does to criticize later Roman society. The misogyny generated and upheld by this discourse is profound.

In helping define and valorize the West as a place of proper masculine dominance, the corrupt Empire discourse contributed to the justification of European domination and the colonial civilizing mission. Like other colonizing discourses, it casts the eastern empire as an object of both repulsion and elicit desire, and the colonial subject served to reinforce the masculinity of the European conqueror.[113] The metaphor of rising and falling of states and civilizations in itself embeds a competition between societies in which the winners are victorious because of their superior merits, which in turn justifies the subjugation of the lesser, declining societies. Adducing the causes of "Byzantine" perpetual decline is an exercise that helps support the worldview that made imperialism and colonialism seem natural and meritorious.

The case for western domination is also made through engineering an historical past that emphasizes the constant growth and innovation of western Europe. By denying, strongly, that "Byzantium" was part of the Roman polity, the whole of Roman history became the heritage of Europe. Nascent Europeans "purified" the corruption of a fallen (western) Roman Empire and soon began state building before they undertook the glorious Renaissance of classical knowledge, fixed Christianity in the Reformation, and moved on to Enlightenment and industrialization. As described above, the break between antiquity and medieval was enforced by claiming the impossibility of a Christian Roman Empire, and the Renaissance was enabled by discounting the classicism of eastern Roman scholars. The corrupt Empire discourse did

---

[113] Anderson and Ivanova, *Is Byzantine Studies a Colonialist Discipline?: Toward a Critical Historiography*, 6.

important work in maintaining this western-centric narrative by transforming the eastern state into a zombie empire, eternally "dead at the core," so decayed and sordid that its existence simply didn't count. Throughout discussions of "Byzantium," the denigration of the East claimed superiority for the West.[114]

Reflections on the Work of "Byzantium"

It is not surprising that different groups we have examined have made different uses of later Roman history. Communities construct meaning in the world around them in dialogue with each other and their perceptions of the world. No one person set forth to divide the Roman Empire into two pieces, one valorized and one denigrated. My goal in dissecting the various meanings imputed to "Byzantium" is not to denigrate those communities and scholars but to understand the impulses and causes that have led to these negative uses of "Byzantium."

Recognizing that "Byzantium" has functioned as a precedent for communism and Orthodox dominion, for enabling visions of racial continuity, and the construction of valorized narratives of Western Civilization, pushes us to consider whether it remains the best way to conceptualize later Roman history. Many of the various agendas that supported the use of "Byzantium" are no longer operative among contemporary academics. Scholars stopped talking about the Dark Ages over half a century ago and the idea that an enlightened secularism prevailed in antiquity is now seen as downright silly. It is also commonly recognized that this traditional narrative of European superiority served the political purposes of justifying first European colonial domination in the nineteenth and early twentieth centuries and then US support of NATO in the twentieth century. Since decolonization and the end of the Cold War, American classrooms have steadily shifted away from Western Civ courses toward World History, and scholars across the globe have been working on new postcolonial conceptualizations of history.

Most scholars who use "Byzantine" now simply see it as a harmless term of art, part of a technical vocabulary that no longer embeds value judgments. Yet,

---

[114] When, in 1900, Harrison advocated for further study of "Byzantine History," he framed this stance with a heavy dose of European supremacist apologetic: "In pleading for a more systematic study of Byzantine history and civilization in the early Middle Ages, I am far from pretending that it can enter into rivalry with that of Western Europe. I do not doubt that it was a lower type; that neither in State nor in Church, neither in policy nor in arms, in morals, in literature, or in art, did it in the sum equal or even approach the Catholic Feudalism of the West. And assuredly, as the West from the time of Charles and Otto onwards rose into modern life, Eastern Christendom sank slowly down into decay and ruin. My point is simply that this Byzantine history and civilization have been unduly deprecated and unfairly neglected." It is as if the European audience needed to be assured of their own superiority in order to make room for a sympathetic understanding of "Byzantine history." Harrison, *Byzantine History*, 39.

in service to these moribund narratives, "Byzantium" is still considered a separate category from the Roman Empire. The following section will outline some benefits of changing our habits.

3 Reasons for Change

Much is to be gained from adopting the emic vocabulary of the new Romans, not least greater clarity. "Byzantium" is not a freestanding category that makes sense on its own; it must be explained that it exists as a conventional marker for something else – the Roman polity, culture, or people. The first thing students learn about "Byzantium" is that it was actually the continuation of the Roman Empire. In speaking of "Byzantium" to nonspecialist audiences, one must always explain that one is talking about the later eastern Roman Empire, which immediately raises questions about the need for "Byzantium" at all. Museum placards have "Byzantium" in large type, followed by a small-type explanation that "Byzantium" was the later Roman Empire. In every case, the "Byzantine" label adds a layer of obfuscation that must be done away with before the conversation can start. Why not just say you're talking about Romans in the first place?

This habit of introducing a rubric, merely to refute it immediately, is not a logical act but rather a vestige of the occlusion of new Rome in service to narratives of Western Civilization. Vanishingly few scholars today would stand up to be counted among those upholding Western supremacy. And yet, the need to keep later Roman society from disrupting paradigms of Western history continues to prompt allegiance to the terminology of "Byzantium." I do not think that scholars are ill intentioned, but rather highly reluctant to overturn the applecart. I want us to look clearly at the applecart we are steadying and consider carefully what our actions are sustaining. The reluctance of Byzantinists to be disruptive may well make us some of the last stalwarts pasting together a nineteenth-century conception of European history.

Changing our terminology may improve the quality of our research by disengaging more fully from the various schematizations of history that "Byzantium" was designed to uphold. To see possible areas of change, we need only think through the implications of the functions of "Byzantium" discussed in the previous chapter. We need to do the work of consciously shaking off this intellectual heritage and reorienting ourselves to let alternative narratives emerge from the materials we study.

Recognizing that "Byzantium" served to enable visions of racial and ethnic continuity across the ages focuses attention on the ways that human communities were described and constructed in different cultures. Understanding varying conceptions of human difference is one of the most pressing questions in the contemporary academy. Many scholars across multiple fields are working to understand how humans come to see themselves as different from each other. The shift from communities conceiving of themselves as Greeks to Romans and then to Greeks again is one of the clearest and most striking examples of a systematic shift in cultural self-understanding on historical record. It is all the more fascinating that these shifts took place without a change in population, and while retaining tremendous continuities in culture and language. How is it that the history of identity changes in the long Roman Empire remains an understudied subject in our era? Our field has been sorely abused by the discourse of "Byzantium," which has obscured this phenomenon from broader historical study.

Insofar as "Byzantium" is deeply enmeshed in the politics of nostalgia for Orthodox dominion, and indeed, Russian imperialism, moving to a new vocabulary will distance our explorations of the past from these contemporary political uses. In those cultural contexts in which enthusiasm for "Byzantium" is equated with religious conservatism, opposition to open and democratic societies, and the revival of an imagined Orthodox hegemony, dropping that terminology has the potential to free academic inquiry from those political constraints and presuppositions.

Recognizing the ways in which the severing of "Byzantium" from the pre-Christian Roman Empire serves to raise Christianity to world-defining status prods us to reassess the significance of that religious change in schemas of human history. Working through the implications of reuniting the two halves of the Roman polity, across that religious change, can help in the larger project of understanding a global past without making the particularity of Christian history definitional for the whole. Studying the history of Roman imperial religion, as a whole, crossing over the moment of Christianization, would provide valuable new perspectives on the history of Orthodoxy. Scholars who assume that all "Byzantine" religion is Orthodoxy see everything that looks like the modern version of that religion, and are blind to everything that does not fit those patterns. They commonly miss aspects of medieval Roman religion that function like classical Roman religion because they begin their studies in the fourth century. This leaves the extremely provocative and illuminating scholarship developed for the study of pre-Christian Roman religion on the shelf unopened. There is no doubt that propositional theology underwent a thorough change with Christianization, but as formal theology is but one aspect of religious practice, the theological shift does not justify cutting the subject of Roman religion into two incommunicable halves.

Exploring the history of the long Roman Empire further troubles the ancient/medieval/Renaissance tripartite division of history. Scholars working in the fields of late antiquity, medieval, and early modern European history have been working on precisely this issue for generations, with the result that it is simply not operative among contemporary historians. Whatever the political changes, the cultural evolution from ancient to late antique, to early and late medieval, to early modern culture was far more a matter of gradual transformation than sudden rupture. The nineteenth-century schematization of sharp breaks between classical, medieval, and Renaissance has been long abandoned. On this issue, the Byzantinists are the holdouts, keeping alive the old schema by maintaining the division between Roman and "Byzantine" history.

The severing of the field of classics from later Roman history has been deleterious to both. Classicists have missed many centuries of commentary and creative uses of their favorite texts by later Roman authors. Byzantinists have too often missed meaningful interactions with classical texts. Both fields are working on recovering from these problems as classicists embrace reception studies and Byzantinists continue to enrich interpretations of their texts through study of ancient connections. Yet we have far more to be gained through the thorough integration of these artificially separated fields.

Considering Roman patterns and mechanisms of imperial succession from Augustus Caesar (31 BCE to 14 CE) through Constantine XII (1449–53 CE) allows the norms and outliers of the system to be more readily apparent and hence provides greater insight into Roman political history. Scholars have tended to take western medieval dynastic kingship as an implicit comparison with the contemporaneous Roman emperors, treating the emperors like kings with the expectation that familial dynastic succession ought to have been the norm. Considering the unity of the Roman polity highlights the peculiar characteristics of imperial succession: the extraordinary stability of the political structure coupled with a short regnal period on average, the creation of fictive dynasties through adoption, acceptance of deposition, and openness to dynastic change. The only effort to examine this system as a whole concluded that it was a form of Republic through right of deposition.[115] This position is certainly open for a fruitful debate, but merely holding dynastic kingship as the norm for all medieval states, and then saying that the "Byzantines" were bad at it, is not, in my view, an intellectually responsible option.

Exploring the whole of Roman history, while consciously rejecting the misogyny of the corrupt Empire discourse, may provide significant insights into the actual gender cultures of Roman society. Looking at the norms and modes of Roman politics without the misogynistic denigration of "Byzantine intrigue" or the fetishization of powerful women as objects of fascination and

---

[115] Kaldellis, *The Byzantine Republic: People and Power in New Rome*.

revulsion will help us understand the medieval evidence for this political culture more clearly. This is not an area in which I believe scholars can claim that the corrupt Empire discourse is no longer operative. Judging by the hate mail I receive for suggesting that Anna Komnene did not want to murder her brother,[116] some people really want "Byzantine" women to be bloodthirsty schemers. Insofar as the corrupt Empire discourse upholds misogyny and heteronormative patriarchy, dismantling it may help us envision more free and open societies. The new appreciations of Roman gender cultures may trouble ideas of masculinity and shed light on the ongoing exultation of strong men in contemporary politics.

On a more practical level, scholars interested in the history of women in politics have so far studied either Livia and Julia Mamaea *or* Pulcheria and Eirene, all the while lamenting the lack of evidence. If the topic were women in politics in the whole Roman Empire, the relevant examples more than double, with obvious benefits. Research derived from the study of one influential mother can more easily help elucidate another if they are not artificially divided into different academic fields.

Another advantage to changing our nomenclature is that it can call attention to the great research being done in Byzantine studies. Pointing out possible avenues of improvement is entirely compatible with upholding the great value of the current research done on later Roman history. Our field is flourishing in the quality and depth of academic projects. The discourse of "Byzantium" has functioned to get it out of the way of dominant narratives of Western Civilization and this terminology continues to make "Byzantine studies" seem disconnected and isolated from the rest of history. Dropping that nomenclature can call attention to the excellent and fascinating research being done in the field. This work of disentangling the study of the *whole* of the Roman polity from the traditional historical narratives that have constrained "Byzantine studies" has the power to reveal fully the fruitfully disruptive capacity of later Roman history.

Eastern Roman history is among the most potentially powerful fields of historical inquiry precisely because striving to understand this culture and society forces us to think in new ways. To help substantiate this claim, I would like to pause briefly to consider some of the reasons for studying history. Many historians work with an intention to explain and understand how the world we live in came to be the way that it is. They unearth the ways that past decisions have created systems that constrain and enable the well-being of our communities. This is undoubtedly one of the meritorious purposes

---

[116] Neville, *Anna Komnene: The Life and Work of a Medieval Historian*.

of history in our society. The dominance of this endeavor, however, sometimes overshadows another primary function of history, which is to help us conceive of change in our world through the examination of communities and societies that were different in some way from our current situation. This is sometimes crudely done when historians desire to find precedents for the changes they want to make to their own communities. The real value, as I see it, is rather to use history to show you examples of ways of thinking and getting along with other humans that you have *not* already thought of and would never think of. History of the distant past, honestly undertaken, offers us examples of things we never would think up: it is profoundly strange, and surprising. It is the surprise of the past that gives us most value because it exposes what we think of as natural to be a matter of historical contingency. It is when we struggle, with difficulty, to understand people who simply do not make any sense to us that we become aware of how much of what we perceive as natural or logical is in fact bounded by our own culture and society. Historical study, so undertaken, gives us true freedom of thought and the ability to envision new futures.

Yet the discourse of "Byzantium" significantly dampens this powerful use of history because it tames the wild otherness of later Roman society and culture and pushes it into the cage of preconceived ideas about what the "Byzantines" were. When we approach the topic with a previously established set of parameters and push the material to fit that framework, we are not giving the material the opportunities to disrupt our understandings of the past. The later Romans are a perfect case for exploring radical alterity because – from their gender cultures to their theories of art, and everything in between – they are wildly unfamiliar and surprising. Additionally, their history busts up some of our most commonly assumed structures of historical periodization and trajectory. For those looking for different patterns of human experience, studying later Romans is extraordinarily powerful and valuable. Confronting all the ways that east Roman history does not fit within the standard narrative of Western Civilization allows it to mess with our minds. This is one of the beautiful things that history can do: it can shake us up and surprise us.

Counterarguments

A good many scholars have already changed their terminology and have largely stopped talking about "Byzantium." Others however defend, sometimes vigorously, the use of this traditional nomenclature. I see three basic types of arguments in favor of "Byzantium." Some scholars actively prize the "Byzantine" label, some have objections to using "Roman," and some believe that change will cause confusion.

While I endeavor to make a strong case for moving away from the "Byzantine" terminology, I want to explicitly honor the choices of scholars who may disagree. This is a call to thoughtfulness, not a mandate to get in line. It is certainly not an attempt to blame or shame scholars who have used, or choose to continue to use, "Byzantine." There is a great deal of variety in the social and academic contexts in which scholarship takes place in our world, and solutions that are viable in one community will not work the same way in another. I am working in a large public university in a predominantly rural region in the middle of the United States, and my views are shaped by the political and economic circumstances affecting scholarship in this context. I readily acknowledge that scholars working in other cultures and places may come to different conclusions. I hope this Element will prompt everyone to reflect on their choices and consciously choose the optimal terminology for describing their work in their context, whatever that may be. I have been privileged to have conversations with scholars who have argued in favor of keeping "Byzantine," and I have endeavored to give those viewpoints due consideration. In the interest of prompting consideration and change, rather than defensiveness, I have chosen not to footnote the arguments that I oppose in the following discussion. Calling out specific scholars for voicing traditional positions seems unnecessarily caustic.

Arguments from Appreciation of "Byzantine"

In Orthodox diaspora communities in the United States, "Byzantium" often is remembered fondly as part of Orthodox history or Greek history. Within Greek heritage communities, churches frequently form the chief locus for the preservation of cultural distinctiveness, offering Greek-language classes for children and holding summertime "Greek festivals" with traditional food and music. In these communities, "Byzantine" music is Orthodox church music. This use of the term tightly codes "Byzantine" as an aspect of Greek culture, and some people feel that moving away from "Byzantium" is a lessening or denigration of their culture.

Cultural and personal commitments to conceptions of heritage are welcome sources of interest in historical research and should be respectfully encouraged. Interest in the field stemming from community engagement may justify using "Byzantine" in some contexts. At the same time, received assumptions can cloud investigation, and so switching to vocabulary of east Roman studies may provide a welcome and clarifying distance from the subject that has been given religious meaning. Insofar as Orthodox heritage communities conceive of "Byzantium" as the glory age of medieval Orthodox dominion, their perceptions of that polity are colored by their current religious and political stances.

Thinking of "Byzantium" as Orthodox history may complicate appreciating the change in religion over time and may overemphasize the importance of religion in that society. Equating later Roman history with Greek Orthodox history is a limiting viewpoint.

Turkish Byzantinists currently work in the context of an Islamicist regime that wishes to repress memory of non-Turkish, and especially Christian, history within the territory of modern Turkey. For them, the use of "Byzantine" is an act of resistance that insists upon acknowledging the Christian history that is under attack. Within state-sponsored visions of history, the "Ionian" and "Roman" eras were periods of foreign conquest that separated Hittite Turkish history from Seljuk Turkish history. In this context, using "Roman" allows Christian history to be more easily dismissed and ignored. Dropping the term "Byzantine" seems like caving to the pressure to erase Christian history from Turkish history. These scholars are fighting Islamicist strands of Turkish society that fear "Byzantium" as an effort to revive the Greek *megali idea* of the reconquest of Istanbul, even though there currently is no Western, or Greek, support for efforts to expand the Greek state at the expense of Turkey. Islamicist politicians wield "Byzantine" as a frightening insult against political opponents. To speak of "Byzantine" history in this context can be a politically provocative pro-Western as well as pluralist stance.

The contingencies of this political situation mean that the stakes are different for scholars working in Turkey than most other places. The scholars directly involved need to work out the optimum vocabulary that will enable them to work both in safety and with maximal impact. The work of insisting upon the recognition of the Orthodox strands in contemporary Turkish heritage and history is vital and significant. It is possible that "Christian Roman" could serve as a strong and clear alternative to "Byzantine" history that would work to resist the erasure of Christian history in Turkey without continuing the problematic discourse of "Byzantium." Given that "Byzantium" is associated with the fear of a revival of the *megali idea,* it is possible that dropping it would help lessen resistance to the study and acknowledgment of the importance of later Roman history for Turkish society and culture.

Arguments against "Roman"

One of the most frequently repeated objections to calling "Byzantines" Romans in western Europe and North America is that identity is complex and that "Roman" was only one aspect of identity. The logical warrant behind this line of reasoning is that calling a group of people by one name denies the ability of those people to simultaneously participate in other groups known by other names. It is objected that calling people Romans minimizes the importance of class differences and religious, regional, and gender identities. Yet precisely because identity is complex, all people participate in multiple group identities. Naming one identity creates no logical impediment to naming others. Nothing about saying that I am an American denies that I am a woman, or a New Yorker, or a bourgeoise professional. Naming the citizens of the later Roman Empire as Romans has no bearing on conversations about the relative importance of religion, class, or gender in their lives.

Another objection is that Roman identity was an elite construct that had little impact on common people. The proposition appears to be factually wrong from an evidentiary standpoint; rather the cultural trend appears to have moved in the opposite direction. Given the high degree of monetization within eastern Roman society, which gave rich and poor alike an opportunity to handle coins minted by the political entity of the Roman state, the ubiquity of contract law conducted under the explicit auspices of that state, and the common images of Emperor Constantine and Helen upholding the True Cross found in many rural churches, it is extremely unlikely that even the most nonelite people are unaware that they were, politically speaking, Roman. Furthermore, from a logical standpoint, even if it were the case that common people were unaware of their political allegiance, the proposition fails to make a case that is preferable to call them by an invented name not used by their more culturally sophisticated contemporaries. Even if it were the case that nonelite people did not consider themselves Romans, that is not a reason to call them Byzantines.

It also has been objected that it is inappropriate to call them Romans because Roman identity was also important to various western European communities. This objection implies that one, and only one, group can have Roman identity at any one time. If this were my claim, then logically, asserting a Roman identity for the East would deny the reality of Roman identity among the Carolingians, for example. Yet the claim that the citizens of the eastern Roman Empire were Romans does not speak to Roman identities among other groups. While the Roman identity of people who wrote books entitled *Gesta Francorum* seems to be of a somewhat different nature than that active in the eastern empire, this is an issue for the scholars of that society to hash out. From the perspective of east Roman history, it is simply off topic. The insistence that scholars of east Rome should not use the term Roman because some of the Franks liked to use that terminology on some days suggests that the discourse of Western supremacy outlined in the previous section may not be as dead as we might like to think.

Some scholars associate the use of the term Roman with the claim that the eastern Romans constituted a nation with a state and then argue that since nations and states are institutions of the modern era, they cannot characterize "Byzantium." The a priori assertion that a medieval community could not be a nation precludes deliberation based on historical evidence. Since that assertion arises from the study of western European national movements, applying it to all societies everywhere throughout time makes European experience the inalterable measure of humanity. The question of whether the medieval Roman community constituted a nation, and their polity a state, ought to be debated based on what we can learn about that society through historical study. We cannot mischaracterize the evidence in order to make that society less disruptive to other historical paradigms. The eastern Roman polity had consistent governmental structures that regulated society according to legal norms and systems that were remarkably resistant to the influence of powerful individuals or families. To say the evidence for this medieval state must be ignored because "real" states are the product of the modern era privileges a particular cultural paradigm of history above what we can truthfully recover from the past. Fundamentally, this line of reasoning holds that when eastern Roman history contradicts European paradigms of state formation, the European paradigm must be preserved at the expense of honest research into later Rome. Once again, the logic of western European history requires that eastern Rome get out of the way and remain safely "Byzantine."

Similarly, some scholars want to continue using "Byzantine" because they do not think that the eastern Romans constituted an ethnicity. Whether a group counts as an ethnicity depends on how one chooses to define that term and its requisites. Different reasonable stances can be taken in this debate over classification. None of them, however, creates reasons to prefer the term "Byzantine." Disagreeing with the scholarly argument that the medieval Romans constituted a distinct ethnic group does not logically lead to the conclusion that it is more accurate to call them Byzantines. Even if a scholar were to conclude that the eastern Romans were not an ethnicity, or a nation, and did not have a state, that would not be a reason for continuing to call them "Byzantines." If one were to decide that the ninth-century Franks should not be considered an ethnicity, or nation, or to have a state, would that be a reason for calling them Tournaites? We should call them Franks because that is what they called themselves, just as we ought to call the Romans by their name.

Another line of objection comes from scholars upholding the view that the "Byzantine Empire" was a "multi-ethnic state." This phrase, popularized in the 1950s and 1960s, worked to emphasize the importance of Armenian, Georgian, Syrian, and Slavic people within the medieval Roman Empire. When scholars began to use the phrase "multi-ethnic state," "Byzantium" was seen as the Greek Empire and their contribution was to highlight that this Greek Empire also included significant numbers of other ethnicities. "Byzantium" was extolled for its cosmopolitan nature that allowed for the integration of Armenians, Egyptians, Syrians, and the other ethnic groups.

The scholars now upholding the multiethnic model seem to look in the past for the ethnic categories existing in our society now, rather than the categories emerging from the medieval evidence. This view sees ethnicity as stable and wants to acknowledge all of the different ethnic groups that contributed to the "Byzantine" Empire, emphasizing the cosmopolitanism and inclusivity of "Byzantine" society. I agree that this society was accepting of many kinds of difference and included a variety of languages and cultural communities. We need to look for the ways human difference is described in our sources, however, rather than importing modern ethnic categories into the past. Past people were not like us, and we cannot understand them if we ignore the categories they created to describe their world.

The importation of modern ethnic categories into the past allows the multi-ethnic model to become a back door for Greek ethnic continuity. The contemporary proponents of the multiethnic state generally avoid specifying which particular ethnicities they see, preferring to talk generally about "Byzantines." Armenians, Georgians, Syrians, and Slavs are most frequently mentioned as the most prominent minority communities. What ethnicities were everyone else? The term "Byzantine" allows this issue to remain unclear. In this model, eastern Rome contained Armenian Byzantines, Slavic Byzantines, in addition to the vast majority of not otherwise specified "Byzantine" Byzantines.[117] The only answer that makes sense within this schema is that the unmarked, plain-vanilla "Byzantines" were Greeks. If Roman is off the table as an identity, then this polity contained some Syrians, Armenians, Georgians, and a great many Greeks. The multiethnic view thus returns to the view that the Greeks were always Greeks who sometimes thought that they were Romans and opposes acknowledging that communities are constituted and defined through their own self-conception. This gives modern conceptions of ethnic difference primacy over the attestations of medieval evidence.

As politics have changed, ethnic chauvinism and nationalism have come to be seen as significant moral problems responsible for horrible violence. The writings of both Fallmerayer and Finlay are seen as distastefully racist, and therefore bad, by most contemporary readers. This repudiation of ethnic nationalism leads some scholars to object to the emic vocabulary of the Romans on the grounds that this creates new ethnicity. Those who wish to end conflicts based on nationalism want to look at the medieval era that had less nationalism in it. Acknowledging that the Romans were Romans, in this

---

[117] Kaldellis, *Romanland: Ethnicity and Empire in Byzantium*, xi–xii, 42–44.

view, means that we have yet another proto-nationalism in the Middle Ages. It is easy to get frustrated with the amount of nineteenth- and twentieth-century scholarship that seems to have been undertaken in service of building various national histories, often at the expense of distorting historical evidence. Yet calls to deny the Romanness of the Romans on the grounds that we do not want to see yet one more ethnic category in the Middle Ages are overt attempts to make the past conform to our desires. This again imposes ideas of what we *want* to have happened onto the past and denies the ability of the past to surprise and unsettle us.

Concern with Confusion

A different set of objections is made on practical grounds. Some scholars, appreciating that "Byzantine studies" is seen as an obscure field, worry that changing the name would be confusing and could jeopardize funding. Our audience and funding streams are already so meagre, this line of thought goes, that we cannot risk losing any more. In countries where university funding is tied to preexisting fields, there is a strong disincentive to change any scholarly nomenclature. I sympathize with scholars working within these systems and urge them to call their subject whatever they need to secure their next paycheck. We can lament, however, that these institutions have frozen a single, late nineteenth-century conception of humanity's research enterprise and seem intent on constraining the evolution of scholarship.

The number of universities that have dedicated lines of faculty and research funding for "Byzantine studies" are dwarfed by the number of educational institutions that do not. In the United States, in the absence of "Byzantine Studies" units, scholars are scattered across departments of Classics, Art History, Religion, History, English, and at least one in Computer Science. Within many of these institutions, funding goes to the fields that generate the most interest among students and, to a lesser extent, to faculty with the most impressive publication records. In these highly competitive environments, fields thrive when classrooms are full, and for classrooms to fill, students need have some sort of idea of what a class is about.

The idea that abandoning "Byzantine" risks losing potential students and funding assumes that there is indeed a market for things "Byzantine," which is not the case in many communities. The name "Byzantine" – which again in English means harmful and dream-killing obstruction – does not provide clear guidance to our topic. The term "Byzantine" cannot be saved by virtue of its semantic clarity. When once I told an engineering professor in a university committee meeting that I study Byzantine history, he blankly asked if that covered university administration. To my surprise, he wasn't joking but rather grasping at anything that could make sense of my statement. "Byzantine" in Wisconsin is an empty signifier aside of the negative adjective.

Conversely, the terminology I am arguing for is among the most widely known and popular premodern historical subjects. In my experience, classes on "Long Roman Empire" fill almost instantaneously, whereas those on "Byzantine History" lag behind department averages. I now tell professors in other fields that I study Roman history and they nod appreciatively. If they ask follow-up questions, my explanations of twelfth-century culture are greeted as fascinating and satisfy the itch for whatever is expected from "Roman history."

While it is impossible to maintain that "Byzantine" is a more easily understood or appealing field than later Roman Studies within the contexts in which I work, there are communities across the globe that do have preconceptions about what the field of "Byzantine studies" contains. Particularly in communities with significant Orthodox Christian heritages, people have heard of Byzantium and believe they have a good understanding of what that term means. In Orthodox heritage communities, it is commonly known that the "Byzantine Empire" was an extension of the Roman Empire and that "the Byzantines thought they were Romans." When I talk to people in these communities about east Roman history, they are not confused and indeed frequently congratulate me, blonde as I am, for knowing that the Byzantines were really Romans. In these circles, using "Roman" may be surprising, but not genuinely confusing. Although it has some meaning, "Byzantine" comes with presuppositions that can inhibit clear observation.

A further charge of sowing confusion has been laid against the project of breaking up with "Byzantium" by scholars who think the concept of a medieval Roman Empire is confusing because the Roman Empire was a classical state that ended before the Middle Ages. I have heard this argument most often from western medievalists who emphatically declare that my usage is too confusing and that I must leave their understanding of the Roman Empire untouched. This is yet another case of a paradigm derived from western European history being used to insist that east Rome cannot have been what it was. These scholars recognize that it is highly disruptive for me to talk about a Roman Empire alive and kicking in the twelfth century, but rather than letting that change the structures of their historical conceptions, they demand that I stop it and go play in the "Byzantine" sandbox.

This last example is the sort of confusion our field should not be afraid of causing. For too long "Byzantinists" have docilely limited their subject to the bounds allowed it by dominant European historical paradigms. If our work is confusing to western medievalists, they should develop a growth mindset and think harder. Dutifully talking about "Byzantium" to avoid disrupting the dominant narrative of western history not only continues to uphold that narrative but also has scholars replaying the colonial dynamics by which the westerners dominate and control the passive easterners. People with doctorates in history are smart enough to do better than this. A great many western medievalists are engaged in trying to rethink and rework their field for a postcolonial, post-Eurocentric world. These scholars would delight in the sort of disruption that new Roman studies, freed of "Byzantium," would provide.

Alternatives and Practicalities

Readers who have been convinced by the basic argument so far may still feel at a loss as to what terminology will be sufficiently precise for their research. We need our books to be found in catalogs and databases, and we need people to know what we are talking about. Different terms will be more or less felicitous for different subfields and topics and likely not one alternative will be fitting in all cases.

Continuing to list "Byzantine" and "Byzantium" among the keywords and search terms with which we can tag our books and articles is certainly sensible. It is already a common practice to list multiple spellings of medieval names as keywords to catch readers who are looking for Nicephorus rather than Nikephoros. Similarly, working "Byzantine" into book subtitles will likely make sense for a long time. We do not want to lose those few readers who are looking for scholarship on "Byzantium." We spend most of our time, however, talking to each other in highly specialized conferences and journal articles. Once you are in a room with people studying twelfth-century epigrams, you all know what you are talking about. You do not have to use "Byzantine" in this context to avoid causing confusion. Rather, you could likely increase precision by talking about Greek-language epigrams, or Constantinopolitan epigrams, for example. Similarly, if you publish an article in *Byzantinische Zeitschrift* and you refer to Leo the Deacon as a Roman historian, no one is going to think you have discovered a new first-century Latin author. The clarification that our current subject used to be called "Byzantine studies" is extremely important at those moments in which our work interfaces with nonspecialists, but this is done easily with a few words and then can be dropped for the duration of the study. It does not justify using "Byzantine" continuously in specialized scholarship.

A clarifying adjective may be needed to distinguish which era and/or end of Roman history is meant. Options that have been coming into use include "medieval Roman," "later Roman," "East Roman," Romanía, and "New Roman." I would add "Christian Roman" to the list of options. Any of these could be the best word in a given context. Uniformity in clarifying adjectives is not necessary either among scholars or within a single scholar's work.

A number of scholars are dissatisfied with using "medieval" because it keeps the western European schematization of history alive. It continues to point to a division of the world into separate ancient and medieval eras. A strong case can be made that Byzantinists should not take up a term that the medievalists are trying to drop. On the other hand, it is useful as a temporal shorthand in scholarship that moves back-and-forth across the whole span of the Roman polity, in which the "classical Empire" is repeatedly contrasted with the "medieval Empire." This works as a temporal designation, as with "medieval China," not an assertion that Roman society or culture was in some way similar to that of medieval Europe.

"East Roman" has the significant advantage of potentially referring to both pre- and post-Christian history in the Roman east, and hence repairing some of the work of "Byzantine." Particularly for scholars doing work that crosses between the western and eastern Mediterranean, "East Roman" and "West Roman" may be the best pairing. Some scholars object that eastern Roman can still be seen as Orientalizing, casting the eastern polity as a lesser adjunct to the real thing. Yet when paired with West Roman, this objection becomes less significant. As a new potential name for the field, "East Roman Studies" has advantages.[118]

"Later Roman" has the advantage of avoiding the potentially orientalizing "East Roman" designation, and the problematic "medieval," but lacks specificity given how many centuries of Roman history are considered "late." Classicists use this term to refer to the fourth and fifth centuries. In scholarship dealing with the history of religion over time, "Christian Roman" and "pre-Christian Roman" may be the best pairing.

The emic term Romanía is probably the most accurate, but the existence of the Transylvanian state of Romania puts a lot of weight on an accent. "New Roman" similarly has the advantage of using terminology developed by Constantine and used fairly regularly thereafter. If this usage catches on and becomes more familiar, it may be the best option. At the time of writing, its meaning is less immediately clear than some of the other contenders.

There are a great many cases in which a political designation is not the most apt. Manuscripts may be better described as Greek language unless there is a clear indication of the political affiliation of the copyist. Objects such as textiles, whose production and use may cross over cultural and political lines, are likely better described through reference to century and material. Icons,

---

[118] Kaldellis, *The Case for East Roman Studies*.

church decoration, hymns, or sermons may be best described as Orthodox. There is room for much more specificity than our current practice of calling everything "Byzantine" allows. Part of changing habits of nomenclature is thinking through what it is exactly that you are studying.

Conclusions

Integrity is achieved by having an alignment between one's actions, thoughts, words, and values. Integrity feels good because it is a consequence of freedom and empowerment within a society that allows people to be who they are, think what they think, and do what they do without contradiction. Integrity is rare in our world where multiple diverse pressures push us to give lip service to ideas and actions we find silly, useless, or harmful. Integrity is also a habit. Therefore, it is worth trying to speak and act with integrity in all those realms that are within our control.

Given the advantages of a life of integrity, why would one choose to lie about something so fundamental as the name of the people one studies? If one is living in a political environment in which freely writing about the past is prescribed behavior, and scholarship must conform to political ideology, scholars should use the words that will help keep them safe. Most scholars working today do not enounter people twisting their arms to talk about "Byzantines" rather than Romans. Much more likely, many more of the people in their lives will understand what it is that they do if they use a vocabulary that does not derive from various nineteenth-century agendas.

At this point many readers may want to insist that talking about "Byzantines" is not a lapse of integrity because it is not a lie. Well, is it true? Talk of truth makes some scholars squeamish, but humans fundamentally interact with the world by drawing inferences based on observation and striving to increase the accuracy of their observations and inferences. When a text mentions *tes ton Romaion basileias ta skeptra*, "the scepters of the empire of the Romans," is the most reasonable inference that it is talking about a "Byzantine" Empire?[119] No: Such a conclusion is willfully inaccurate enough to count as dishonest and not *true*. If you are dealing with those sources from seventh-century Italy or fifteenth-century Constantinople that indeed do talk about Byzantines, then obviously using that term would be optimally accurate. In part, it is a commitment to accuracy and truthfulness in history that makes the issue of the nomenclature in our field so significant and pressing. It is because of my commitments to speaking truthfully about the

---

[119] Life of Euthemios the Younger. Greenfield and Talbot, trans., *Holy Men of Mount Athos*, 14.

past that I get irked when people disregard the evidence we have about the past because they prefer to talk about "Byzantines."

The idea that communities and identities are constructed socially and culturally, and that those constructions can change, sometimes radically, over time is a verifiable, observable reality. The idea that the meaning of texts is constructed in a dialogue between the community of readers and the text is also a verifiable, observable reality. We have an abundance of examples of texts that were interpreted to mean one thing in one century and a rather different thing in a different century. Paying attention to these changes and variations is not abandoning truth; it is observing reality accurately as it changes over time. Practicing theoretically informed modes of analysis increases and enriches the accuracy of our observations without lessening human dependence on inductive reasoning based on observation. Striving for truthfulness thus remains a core commitment of scholarship, and hence my call for integrity is apt.

For me, endeavoring to respect the dignity of every human being is another existentially grounding commitment. I consider regarding other humans with respect as a morally commendable stance. While the dead are no longer around to feel insulted, treating their memory with a lack of respect leaves one practicing being disrespectful. As with integrity, respect is a habit that grows as you practice it. Respect for the dead pushes me to call them Romans, when that is what they called themselves. Respect for my contemporaries means I will appreciate and value your scholarly contributions regardless of whether I have managed to persuade you.

"Byzantium" is now kept alive by Byzantinists, mostly because we have not collectively done the work of figuring out how to handle our subject without reference to the schemas imposed by European history. Obviously, most scholars now are not consciously trying to force "Byzantine" culture into a box made by late nineteenth-century European imperialists. Such an accusation would be absurd, and it is not being made. Rather, most historians work within the established fields and subjects that are already extant within the academy. People embark on studying whatever particular thing they are working on using the nomenclature of their teachers and colleagues. There is nothing nefarious in using the same vocabulary for a field as one's dissertation advisor.

Nonetheless, the academy cannot pretend to be a place of learning and innovative research if we are not able to change our minds and reconceive of our fields. It is fair to ask academic researchers to pause in their daily pursuit of expertise in their subspecialties to think about the rubrics, nomenclature, and fundamental structures of the broader fields. The call to think historically without the discourse of "Byzantium" is a call to profoundly recast the most basic structures of our historical narratives. The discourse of "Byzantium" persists, not just out of habit, but because insisting on an alternative is extremely disruptive of so many of our basic historical paradigms. This intellectual project is not simple but has the potential to force a fruitful reworking of the fundamental schematization of Eurasian history that will reverberate far beyond the boundaries of traditional "Byzantine Studies."

Bibliography

Amanpour, Christiane, and Walter Isaacson. "Interview with Former U.S. Ambassador to NATO and Former U.S. Special Representative for Ukraine Negotiations Kurt Volker." *Amanpour*, June 26, 2023.

Anderson, Benjamin, and Mirela Ivanova, eds. *Is Byzantine Studies a Colonialist Discipline?: Toward a Critical Historiography*. The Pennsylvania State University Press, 2023.

Ando, Clifford. *Imperial Ideology and Provincial Loyalty in the Roman Empire*. University of California Press, 2000.

The Matter of the Gods: Religion and the Roman Empire. University of California Press, 2008.

Appiah, Anthony. *The Lies That Bind: Rethinking Identity, Creed, Country, Color, Class, Culture*. Liveright, 2018.

Aschenbrenner, Nathanael and Jake Ransohoff, eds., *The Invention of Byzantium in Early Modern Europe*. Dumbarton Oaks, 2021.

Barnett, S. J. *The Enlightenment and Religion: The Myths of Modernity*. Manchester University Press, 2003.

Beard, Mary, John A. North, and Simon R. F. Price. *Religions of Rome*. Cambridge University Press, 1998.

Berkowitz, Steve. "NCAA Facing New 'Pay-for-Play' Challenges in Lawsuit." *Press – Citizen*, December 9, 2023. 2899554021. U.S. Newsstream.

Boston Globe. "Byzantine Boston Makes It Next to Impossible to Open a Restaurant." July 10, 2022. 2687166746. U.S. Newsstream.

Boston Investigator. "Read, Read! Read!!" October 24, 1860.

Brown, Jeffrey, Jon Frankel, William Brangham et al. "PBS NewsHour for December 26, 2023." *PBS Newshour*, December 26, 2023.

Bury, John Bagnell. *A History of the Later Roman Empire: From Arcadius to Irene. (395 A.D. to 800 A.D.)*. Macmillan, 1898.

Cameron, Averil. *Byzantine Matters*. Princeton University Press, 2014.

Champion, Craige. *The Peace of the Gods: Elite Religious Practices in the Middle Roman Republic*. Princeton University Press, 2017.

Connersville Examiner. "Dying Nations." September 8, 1881.

Curteis, Arthur. *History of the Roman Empire, from the Death of Theodosius the Great to the Coronation of Charles the Great, A.D. 395–800*. Rivingtons, 1875.

Dickinson, Peter. "Putin's New Ukraine Essay Reveals Imperial Ambitions." *Atlantic Council: UkraineAlert*, July 15, 2021. www.atlanticcouncil.org/blogs/ukrainealert/putins-new-ukraine-essay-reflects-imperial-ambitions/.

Drost, Niels, and Beatrice de Graaf. "Putin and the Third Rome: Imperial-Eschatological Motives as a Usable Past." *Journal of Applied History* 4, no. 1–2 (2022): 28–45.

"Dying Nations." In *The Christian Treasury, Containing Contributions from Ministers and Members of Various Evangelical Denominations*, 18:83. Johnston, Hunter, 1862.

Fallmerayer, Jakob Philipp. *Geschichte der Halbinsel Morea während des Mittelalters: ein historischer Versuch*. J.G. Cotta'schen Buchhandlung, 1830.

Field Level Media. "Brittney Griner Plans 'intimate, Moving' Memoir on Imprisonment in Russia." *The Times – Tribune*, April 11, 2023. 2799223662. U.S. Newsstream.

Finlay, George. *A History of Greece: From Its Conquest by the Romans to the Present Time, B.C. 146 to A.D. 1864. Volume 1, Greece under the Romans*. 2nd ed. Vol. 1. 7 vols. Clarendon Press, 1877.

———. *A History of Greece : From Its Conquest by the Romans to the Present Time, B.C. 146 to A.D 1864. Volume 2, The Byzantine Empire, Part I*. 2nd ed. Clarendon Press, 1877.

———. *A History of Greece : From Its Conquest by the Romans to the Present Time, B.C. 146 to A.D. 1864. Volume 3, The Byzantine and Greek Empires, Part II*. Vol. 3. 7 vols. Clarendon Press, 1877.

———. *History of the Byzantine and Greek Empires, from DCCXVI to MCCCCLIII*. William Blackwood and Sons, 1854.

Frank, Richard, and Holly Domus. "Byzantine Water Laws Will Leave Californians High and Dry." *Visalia Times – Delta / Tulare Advance – Register*, February 26, 2022. 2633187453. U.S. Newsstream.

Fritze, John. "Special Ed Student Can Sue School: Supreme Court Ruling Could Empower Parents." *USA TODAY*, March 23, 2023. 2789555819. U.S. Newsstream.

Georgetown Courier. "Dying Nations." June 22, 1882.

Gibbon, Edward. *History of the Decline and Fall of the Roman Empire*. Luke White, 1788.

Greenfield, Richard P. H., and Alice-Mary Maffry Talbot, trans. *Holy Men of Mount Athos*. Harvard University Press, 2016.

Hall's Journal of Health. "Dying Nations." May 1, 1860.

Harrison, Frederic. *Byzantine History in the Early Middle Ages: The Rede Lecture: Delivered in the Senate House, Cambridge, June 12, 1900*. Macmillan, 1900.

Harvey, David Allen. "The Rise of Modern Paganism? French Enlightenment Perspectives on Polytheism and the History of Religions." *Historical Reflections* 40, no. 2 (2014): 34–55.

Hendy, Michael F. *Studies in the Byzantine Monetary Economy, c. 300–1450.* Cambridge University Press, 1985.

"The Economy: A Brief Survey." In *Byzantine Studies: Essays on the Slavic World and the Eleventh Century*, 141–52. Aristide D. Caratzas, 1992.

Herald of Gospel Liberty. "Dying Nations." December 8, 1904.

Holmes, Michael, Matthew Chance, Steve Hall et al. "Pro-War Russian Blogger Killed in Explosion." *CNN Newsroom*, April 3, 2023.

Kaldellis, Anthony. *Hellenism in Byzantium: The Transformations of Greek Identity and the Reception of the Classical Tradition.* Cambridge University Press, 2007.

The Byzantine Republic: People and Power in New Rome. Harvard University Press, 2015.

Romanland: Ethnicity and Empire in Byzantium. Harvard University Press, 2019.

The Case for East Roman Studies. Arc Humanities Press, 2024.

Kazhdan, Alexander. "Russian Pre-Revolutionary Studies on Eleventh-Century Byzantium." In *Byzantine Studies Essays on the Slavic World and the Eleventh Century*, 111–24. Aristide Caratzas, 1992.

Laiou, Angeliki. *The Economic History of Byzantium from the Seventh through the Fifteenth Century.* Dumbarton Oaks, 2002.

Lecky, William Edward Hartpole. *History of European Morals: From Augustus to Charlemagne.* D. Appleton, 1873.

Marciniak, Przemysław. "Oriental Like Byzantium: Some Remarks on Similarities between Byzantium and Orientalism." In *Imagining Byzantium: Perceptions, Patterns, Problems*, edited by Andreas Gietzen, Christina Hadjiafxenti, and Alena Alshanskaya, 47–54. Byzanz Zwischen Orient Und Okzident 11. Verlag des Römisch-Germanischen Zentralmuseums, 2018.

Maunder, Samuel. *The History of the World: Comprising a General History, Both Ancient and Modern, of All the Principal Nations of the Globe, Their Rise, Progress, Present Condition, Etc.* Vol. 1. H. Bill, 1852.

The History of the World: Comprising a General History, Both Ancient and Modern, of All the Principal Nations of the Globe, Their Rise, Progress, Present Condition, Etc. Vol. 2. H. Bill, 1852.

Mealins, Evan. "Lawsuit Claims Correctional Officers Stabbed, Beat Inmate: TDOC: Wounds Were Self-Inflicted, Accidental." *The Tennessean*, November 4, 2023. 2885705921. U.S. Newsstream.

Mellow, Craig. "Disaster Insurance Gets Lift in Emerging Markets." *Barron's* 103, no. 48 (November 27, 2023): 33.

Milman, Henry Hart. *History of Latin Christianity; including That of the Popes to the Pontificate of Nicolas V.* Vol. 8. 9 vols. J. Murray, 1867.

Montesquieu, Charles de Secondat. *Montesquieu's Considerations on the Causes of the Grandeur and Decadence of the Romans.* Translated by Jehu Baker. D. Appleton, 1882.

Neville, Leonora. *Authority in Byzantine Provincial Society, 950–1100.* Cambridge University Press, 2004.

———. *Heroes and Romans in Twelfth-Century Byzantium: The Material for History of Nikephoros Bryennios.* Cambridge University Press, 2012.

———. *Anna Komnene: The Life and Work of a Medieval Historian.* Oxford University Press, 2016.

———. "Singing with David and Contemplating Agesilaus: Ethical Training in Byzantium." In *The Reception of Greek Ethics in Late Antiquity and Byzantium*, edited by Sophia Xenophontos and Anna Marmodoro, 140–58. Cambridge University Press, 2021.

Nongbri, Brent. *Before Religion: A History of a Modern Concept.* Yale University Press, 2013.

Papaioannou, Stratis, ed. *The Oxford Handbook of Byzantine Literature.* Oxford University Press, 2021.

Putin, Vladimir. "On the Historical Unity of Russians and Ukrainians." Kremlin, July 12, 2021.

Pütz, Wilhelm. *Handbook of Mediaeval Geography and History.* Translated by R. B. Paul. xii, D. Appleton, 1850.

Robbins, Royal. *Outlines of Ancient and Modern History on a New Plan. Embracing Biographical Notices of Illustrious Persons and General Views of Geography, Population, Politics ... of Ancient and Modern Nations.* Vol. 2. Belknap and Hamersley, 1837.

———. *Outlines of Ancient and Modern History on a New Plan. Embracing Biographical Notices of Illustrious Persons and General Views of Geography, Population, Politics ... of Ancient and Modern Nations.* Vol. 1. Belknap and Hamersley, 1837.

Rocoles, Jean Baptiste. *Introduction Generale a l'histoire Prophane: Contenant Son Parfait Usage.* 4th ed. Vol. 2. 2 vols. chez Pierre le Petit ..., Edme Couterot et Charles Angot, 1672.

Scheid, John. *The Gods, the State, and the Individual: Reflections on Civic Religion in Rome.* Translated by Clifford Ando. Empire and After. University of Pennsylvania Press, 2016.

Sharp, Sonja. "Gaps in Care for Eating Disorders; Cases Have Surged, but Long Waits and Byzantine Medi-Cal Rules Stymie the State's Poorest Patients." *Los Angeles Times*, August 14, 2023. 2849774466. US Newsstream.

Smith, Jonathan Z. *Drudgery Divine: On the Comparison of Early Christianities and the Religions of Late Antiquity.* School of Oriental and African Studies, 1990.

Relating Religion: Essays in the Study of Religion. University of Chicago, 2004.

Solomon, Lori. "Prior Authorization Increases Use of Health Care Resources, Physicians Say." *St. Joseph News – Press*, March 15, 2023. 2787025652. US Newsstream.

Stewart, Michael Edward, David Alan Parnell, and Conor Whately, eds., *The Routledge Handbook on Identity in Byzantium.* Taylor and Francis, 2022.

Stroumsa, Guy G. *A New Science: The Discovery of Religion in the Age of Reason.* Harvard University Press, 2010.

Swinton, William. *Outlines of the World's History: Ancient, Mediæval, and Modern: With Special Relation to the History of Civilization and the Progress of Mankind.* Ivison, Blakeman, and Company, 1874.

Taylor, William Cooke. *A Manual of Modern History: Containing the Rise and Progress of the Principal European Nations, Their Political History, and the Changes in Their Social Condition: With a History of the Colonies Founded by Europeans.* 5th ed., D. Appleton, 1847.

The Co-Operative News and Journal of Associated Industry. "Dying Nations." January 8, 1898.

Theodoropoulos, Panagiotis. "Did the Byzantines Call Themselves Byzantines? Elements of Eastern Roman Identity in the Imperial Discourse of the Seventh Century." *Byzantine and Modern Greek Studies* 45, no. 1 (April 2021): 25–41.

Thompson, Lewis. *Nineteen Christian Centuries in Outline. A Guide to Historical Study for Home Reading and Literary Clubs.* A. Craig, 1881.

Vermont Journal. "Dying Nations." March 16, 1861.

Voltaire. *Œuvres Complètes de Voltaire avec des remarques et des notes historiques, scientifiques et littéraires.* Delangle Frères, 1825.

Wall Street Journal (Online). "One Part of British Culture That Didn't Cross the Ocean to America; I'm Amazed How Compliant the Brits Are with Byzantine Regulations Imposed by Their Leaders." March 15, 2023. 2786904419. US Newsstream.

Weber, Georg. *Outlines of Universal History, from the Creation of the World to the Present Time.* xvi, 483, Whittaker, 1851.

Whalin, Douglas. *Roman Identity from the Arab Conquests to the Triumph of Orthodoxy.* Palgrave Macmillan, 2020.

Acknowledgments

I have been thinking about the detachment of "Byzantium" from the Roman Empire since the fall of 1988, when Professor Vasily Rudich ended his introductory Roman history course by calling that divide an inexplicable and bewildering example of academic foolishness that one of us should try to figure out. He then said: "What the world needs most is Byzantinists." He may have meant the *academic* world, but either way, he made working out why people thought Byzantium was separate from Rome seem both vitally important and somehow a plausible career path. The debt I owe him is immense. Early on David Turner helped me see western European secularism as a key reason for believing that Orthodox Byzantium could not be Roman. The indefatigable efforts of Anthony Kaldellis have made it increasingly difficult to ignore how the construct of "Byzantium" is not a logical interpretation of the medieval evidence. This Element can begin with the question of why scholars have preferred to talk about Byzantines because he has made denying they were Romans untenable. I am grateful to them, and to the many other colleagues, students, and teachers with whom I have explored this question.

For Vasily Rudich

Cambridge Elements

Rethinking Byzantium

Leonora Neville
University of Wisconsin-Madison

Leonora Neville is the John and Jeanne Rowe Professor of Byzantine History and Vilas Distinguished Achievement Professor at the University of Wisconsin-Madison. She has written extensively on eastern Roman society, particularly on authority in provincial communities, history writing, gender, and the importance of the classical past for medieval Roman culture.

Darlene Brooks Hedstrom
Brandeis University

Darlene Brooks Hedstrom is the Myra and Robert Kraft and Jacob Hiatt Chair in Christian Studies at Brandeis University. She is an archaeologist and historian of the late antique Mediterranean world. Her works examine the intersection of objects, religious practice, monasticism, and the history of archaeology.

About the Series

Elements in Rethinking Byzantium offer crisp and accessible introductions to vibrant current research on medieval eastern Roman society and culture which sets them within broader schemas of pre-modern history and cultural study. Individual Elements address various aspects of visual and literary cultures, history, and religion in the territory and cultural sphere of the Roman Empire, broadly conceived, from the fourth to fifteenth centuries CE.

Cambridge Elements

Rethinking Byzantium

Elements in the Series

Kyivan Rus in Medieval Europe
Christian Raffensperger

Sailing Away from Byzantium toward East Roman History
Leonora Neville

A full series listing is available at: www.cambridge.org/RTHB

For EU product safety concerns, contact us at Calle de José Abascal, 56–1°, 28003 Madrid, Spain or eugpsr@cambridge.org.

www.ingramcontent.com/pod-product-compliance
Lightning Source LLC
LaVergne TN
LVHW020352260326
834688LV00045B/1683